A VISUAL GUIDE TO
SHAKESPEARE'S LIFE AND TIMES

is the product of extensive research, designed to increase understanding and appreciation of the great Elizabethan dramatist and poet. The vivid commentary, together with the striking illustrations derived from authentic graphic sources, enable the reader to embark on a fascinating journey through the background elements that brought inspiration and lasting popularity to the famous playwright. Here, in the countryside of Stratford, the streets of London and the theatres of the world, the Shakespeare story unfolds in all its magnificence.

A Visual Guide to Shakespeare's Life and Times

by

Louis B. Wright and Elaine W. Fowler

with
the editorial assistance
of Educational Direction, Inc.

WASHINGTON SQUARE PRESS
POCKET BOOKS · NEW YORK

A VISUAL GUIDE TO SHAKESPEARE'S
LIFE AND TIMES

WASHINGTON SQUARE PRESS edition published January, 1975

L

Published by
POCKET BOOKS, a division of Simon & Schuster, Inc.,
630 Fifth Avenue, New York, N.Y.

WASHINGTON SQUARE PRESS editions are distrib-
uted in the U.S. by Simon & Schuster, Inc., 630 Fifth
Avenue, New York, N.Y. 10020, and in Canada by Simon
& Schuster of Canada, Ltd., Markham, Ontario, Canada.

1265

CONTENTS

Preface   vii

1. Shakespeare in Warwickshire   1

2. Young Shakespeare in London   49

3. Shakespeare's Theatre   95

4. Elizabeth I and James I   147

5. The Renaissance   177

6. The Publication of Shakespeare's Plays   209

7. Shakespeare's Return to Stratford   227

   Epilogue: Shakespeare's Reputation   237

PREFACE

The pictorial material reproduced here, gathered in the course of editing the Folger Library General Reader's Shakespeare, published by Washington Square Press, is designed to provide the student with a convenient, portable and inexpensive volume of visual aids to understanding Shakespeare and his times. More elaborate volumes, some reproducing pictures in vivid color, are available on library shelves, but the expense of producing such works places them beyond the reach of most students.

The authors are indebted to the Folger Shakespeare Library and its staff for pictorial material, gathered during the directorship of the senior editor of the present volume. Some are no longer there to know of our gratitude. We are especially grateful to the late Virginia LaMar for her able assistance and research.

Some of the illustrations also appear in *Shakespeare for Everyman* by Louis B. Wright (Washington Square Press) and here and there in the Folger Library General Reader's Shakespeare. All quotations cited in the present volume come from that edition.

Louis B. Wright
Elaine W. Fowler

August 8, 1973

SHAKESPEARE
IN WARWICKSHIRE

A map of Warwickshire published in 1603, believed to be

COMITATVS WARWICENSIS

Præter ciuitatem
Couentriæ et vrbem
Warwici continet Op-
pida Mercatoria XIII.
Ecclesiasque Parychi-
ales CLVIII. Fluuios
VII. et pontes XXI.

LECES TRIAE PARS.

NORT HAMPTO NIAE PARS.

OXONIAE PARS.

SCALA MILIARIVM.

5   10

Warwicum Com. continet in
Printed and sould by I. Sene

Superficie   555.
Circuitu   122
Longitudine   37.
Latitudine   28.

Miliaria

the earliest on which roads were marked. It was based
upon Christopher Saxton's map of 1576 "now corrected and
augmented."

William Shakespeare was born at Stratford-upon-Avon in Warwickshire, it is assumed on Sunday, April 23, 1564. His birth is not recorded, but the date of his baptism at Trinity Church appears in the register for April 26. Since children were usually baptized three days after birth, April 23 has been designated as his birth date.

He was born in a house in Henley Street that, with some modern restoration, looks today much as it did in the poet's boyhood. The earliest known picture of Shakespeare's birthplace is this drawing made by Richard Greene about the year 1762. One side of the house was the business establishment of John Shakespeare, William's father. He tanned leather, made gloves and was a general merchant dealing in wool, grain and other local products.

FROM A DRAWING BY RICHARD GREENE, CA. *1762*, IN HALLIWELL-PHILLIPPS, "ARTISTIC RECORDS." FOLGER LIBRARY.

Shakespeare's birthplace—the earliest known view. Note the similarity of the modern restoration.

COURTESY, THE TRUSTEES OF THE SHAKESPEARE BIRTHPLACE TRUST.

Shakespeare's birthplace today.

When this nineteenth-century sketch was made, Stratford's Trinity Church still looked much as it did at the time of Shakespeare's baptism. The woodcut illustration of a christening in the Church of England dates from Shakespeare's childhood and shows the type of dress worn at the time. Young William was the eldest surviving child, with several younger brothers and sisters.

FROM A WATERCOLOR DRAWING
BY J. C. BUCKLER
(1823), IN HALLIWELL-PHILLIPPS,
"ARTISTIC RECORDS."
FOLGER LIBRARY.

*Trinity Church, Stratford,
from the southeast.*

FROM A WOODCUT ILLUSTRATION IN RICHARD DAY,
A Book of Christian Prayers (1578).
FOLGER LIBRARY.

A baptism scene of the time of Shakespeare's childhood.

Stratford was a busy market town on one of the principal roads to London. On market days Shakespeare as
a child might have been seen on the ledge around the
Market Cross watching the buyers and sellers, for his
father's glove stall was nearby. The picture shows the
Henley Street side, as sketched by John T. Blight in
1864. The woodcut of a glover's and leather dealer's
stall was published in 1568, when Shakespeare was four
years old.

FROM HARTMANN SCHOPPER,
"PANOPLIA" (1568).
FOLGER LIBRARY.

*A glover's and leather work-
er's stall as pictured in a sixteenth-century woodcut.*

FROM A SKETCH BY JOHN T. BLIGHT (1863-64)
AFTER AN EARLIER DRAWING
BY C. F. GREEN (1821).
FOLGER LIBRARY.

The Market Cross, Stratford, from the corner of Wood and Henley streets.

John Shakespeare, a prominent citizen of Stratford, for a time held the post of bailiff (what we would call mayor), and in his official capacities would have dressed much like this. His wife, Mary Arden, had been brought up on a farm at Wilmcote, near Stratford, which has now been restored and offers valuable insights into the rural life that young William observed.

FROM JOHN SPEED,
*Theatrum imperii
Magnae Britanniae* (1616).
FOLGER LIBRARY.

*"A Citizen" of the sixteenth
century.*

FROM AN ETCHING BY
JOHN MAC PHERSON IN
The Land of Shakespeare,
F. G. FLEAY (1889).
FOLGER LIBRARY.

*The family home of Mary
Arden, Shakespeare's mother,
at Wilmcote.*

Stratford, in fact, was the center of a rich farming country, and the future poet could not avoid witnessing scenes that apparently left vivid impressions upon his youthful mind. Indeed, the imagery of his plays and poems reflects many memories of this early period of his life, particularly of dramatic conflict in the animal world.

FROM   FRANCIS   BARLOW,   *Various Birds and Beasts* (CA. 1755).

FOLGER LIBRARY.

What, all my pretty chickens and their dam
At one fell swoop?
(Macbeth *IV. iii. 255-56*)

The vulnerability of love and innocence to the predatory instincts in nature was a major theme of Shakespeare's narrative poems. The large dovecote still visible at the Arden farm would have provided opportunities to observe the affectionate turtledoves billing and cooing, and to see occasional tragedy strike with the sudden dive of a hawk or falcon.

FROM GEORGE VERTUE, *Description of the Works of Wenceslaus Hollar* (1759).

FOLGER LIBRARY.

Doves billing and cooing.

This said, he shakes aloft his Roman blade,
Which, like a falcon tow'ring in the skies,
Coucheth the fowl below with his wings' shade,
Whose crooked beak threats if he mount he dies.
So under his insulting falchion lies
   Harmless Lucretia, marking what he tells
   With trembling fear, as fowl hear falcons' bells.

(*The Rape of Lucrece* 505–11)

In the gathering twilight of a small boy's bedtime,
flights of gloomy crows making for the trees later evoked
the chilling lines:

Light thickens, and the crow
Makes wing to the rooky wood.

(*Macbeth* III. ii. 55-56)

FROM ARNOLD FREITAG, *Mythologia ethica* (1579).
FOLGER LIBRARY.

A hawk with a captured dove.

In this crude drawing from a pictorial commonplace book, the man armed with the bow and arrow is keeping crows away from freshly sown seed.

FROM THOMAS TREVELYON, "A PICTORIAL
COMMONPLACE BOOK" (1608).
FOLGER LIBRARY.

Farmers protecting their seed from crows.

The dark and foreboding atmosphere of *Macbeth* was further enhanced by evoking the sounds of nocturnal creatures after dark, as in:

> It was the owl that shrieked, the fatal bellman
> Which gives the stern'st good-night.
>
> (II. ii. 5–6)

> Ere the bat hath flown
> His cloistered flight, ere to black Hecate's summons
> The shard-borne beetle with his drowsy hums
> Hath rung night's yawning peal. . . .
>
> (III. ii. 44–47)

FROM BARLOW, *Various Birds.*
FOLGER LIBRARY.

An owl and other woodland birds.

FROM ULISSE ALDROVANDI,
Ornithologiae (1599–1603).
FOLGER LIBRARY.

Views of bats in flight.

Scenes from Trinity Church, which he was required to attend as a child, also left vivid impressions which we find later reflected in Shakespeare's plays. Gravediggers in the churchyard must have had a macabre fascination for him; in *Hamlet* the gravedigger tossing up the skull of Yorick echoes countless scenes that Shakespeare apparently witnessed in the overcrowded graveyard at Stratford. We have only to recall that his father was a leather dresser, as we hear:

> Hamlet: How long will a man lie i' the earth ere he rot?
> Clown: Faith, if he be not rotten before he die . . . he will last you some eight year or nine year. A tanner will last you nine year.
> Hamlet: Why he more than another?
> Clown: Why sir, his hide is so tanned with his trade that he will keep out water a great while.
>
> (*Hamlet* V. i. 157–64)

Trinity Church, like many other churches in this period, had a charnel house for the preservation of bones unearthed as gravediggers prepared fresh graves. Trinity's charnel house, abutting on the northeast side of the church, is visible in this view. Shakespeare's memory of

Trinity Church, Stratford, from the north, showing the charnel house at the east end of the chancel. This is one of the earliest known views of the church.

Seventeenth-century gravediggers.

such a charnel house is evident in some of his allusions and descriptions, as, for example, in Macbeth's reaction to the ghost of Banquo:

> If charnel houses and our graves must send
> Those that we bury back, our monuments
> Shall be the maws of kites.
>
> (*Macbeth* III. iv. 87–89)

FROM A SKETCH BY SAUNDERS (CA. 1820) AFTER
AN EARLIER DRAWING, IN HALLIWELL-PHILLIPPS,
"ARTISTIC RECORDS."
FOLGER LIBRARY.

Interior of the charnel house.

Before going to grammar school, young William would have received early instruction at home, in family gatherings much like this one. He would have learned his letters from a hornbook—a paper sheet giving the ABC's and a few sentences, usually from the Bible, fixed on a small wooden paddle and covered by a thin sheet of transparent horn to protect the page. There was no protection, however, against loss, then as now a persistent plague of schoolboy and teacher. In *The Two Gentlemen of Verona* Shakespeare compares a lover's sigh to that of "a schoolboy that had lost his ABC" (II. i. 24–25). The rare survival shown here, a hornbook dating from about 1550, is old enough to have been lost by young William himself.

FROM A WOODCUT ILLUSTRATION IN
The Whole Book of Psalms (1563).
FOLGER LIBRARY.

Family instruction.

FOLGER LIBRARY.

A hornbook of about 1550.

The grammar school at Stratford, available to John Shakespeare's family, had an excellent reputation and boasted learned schoolmasters whom the dramatist may later have caricatured in *Love's Labor's Lost* and elsewhere. In such schools, an Elizabethan youth got most of his basic education. The grammar schools provided a thorough grounding in Latin literature, and some taught Greek. The Stratford Grammar School, pictured here, is still in use, with some desks that date from Shakespeare's time—much carved with names and initials of former students. The Director of the Birthplace Trust is still hoping to find the initials "WS" carved on some desk. Shakespeare, perhaps, was too smart to leave such evidence of misbehavior because of the severity of schoolmasters in his time.

*The Stratford Grammar School today, scarcely changed since
Shakespeare's time.*

*An Elizabethan classroom. Note the switches under the
schoolmaster's chair.*

FROM ALEXANDER NOWELL, *A Catechism* (1593).
FOLGER LIBRARY.

With the help of "Lily's Latin Grammar," a textbook so enduring that it ran through twenty-one editions between 1557 and 1640 and continued to be used by settlers in colonial America, Shakespeare and his contemporaries read some poetry of Ovid and maybe a Latin play by Plautus or Terence. Shakespeare probably remembered having read Plautus' *Menaechmi,* a comedy about mistaken identity of twins, when he sat down to write *The Comedy of Errors.* He later used material from Ovid's *Metamorphoses* and other works.

We may guess, from certain well-known lines, that young William had as much aversion to school as the next boy:

> Then the whining schoolboy, with his satchel
> And shining morning face, creeping like snail
> Unwillingly to school.
>
> (*As You Like It* II. vii. 155–57)

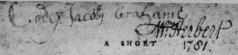

A SHORT

INTRODVCTION OF

GRAMMAR GENERALLIE

TO BE VSED. COMPILED AND
SET FORTH, FOR THE BRIN-
GYNG VP OF ALL THOSE THAT
INTEND TO ATTAINE THE
KNOVVLEGE OF THE
LATIN TONGVE.

✥◑✳◐✥

⁎

PSAL. CXIX.

Wherby shall a Childe clense and amende his waie?
By ruling himselfe accordinge to thy worde, o Lorde.

Intime truth cometh to light, id prevaileth.

Redemi the time, for the daies are euill.

CVM PRIVILEGIO.

M. D. LVII.

The title page of A Short Introduction of Grammar Generally to Be Used, *by William Lily and John Colet (1557), better known as "Lily's Latin Grammar."*

The. xv. Bookes

of P. Ouidius Naso, entytuled

Metamorphosis, translated oute of
Latin into English meeter, by Ar-
thur Golding Gentleman,
A worke very pleasaunt
and delectable.

With skill, heede, and iudgement, this worke must be read,
For else to the Reader it standes in small stead.

15   67.

Imprynted at London, by
Willyam Seres.

The title page of Arthur Golding's translation of Ovid's
Metamorphoses (1567). The bear and ragged staff was the
device of the Earl of Leicester, owner of Kenilworth Castle
near Stratford, to whom the book was dedicated.

MENAECMI.

¶ A pleasant and fine Con-
ceited Comædie, taken out of the most excellent wittie Poet *Plautus* :

Chosen purposely from out the rest, as least harmefull, and
yet most delightfull.

Written in English, by *VV. VV.*

LONDON
Printed by Tho. Creede,

and are to be sold by William Barley, at his
shop in Gratious streete.

1 5 9 5.

The title page of the first English translation in print of
Plautus's Menaechmi *(1595).*

When school was out, young William, now old enough to wander and explore on his own, would have learned of the world beyond Stratford and the Arden farm. Warwickshire was—and still is—a beautiful county, with rolling hills, dark woods, waving fields of grain and green pasture land. It retains the charm that Shakespeare knew and often described in his plays, even when the purported scene might be called a "Wood near Athens" or an "Orchard in Verona."

FROM A PHOTOGRAPH. COURTESY, L. B. WRIGHT.

The Warwickshire countryside today.

Warwickshire actually had a Forest of Arden, which lay to the north of Stratford. It was natural that Shakespeare would remember and use the name when he came to describe the rural scenes of *As You Like It*. Despite olive trees and lionesses, the atmosphere of the play is unmistakably Warwickshire woodland, where, like the young men of the play, a boy might "fleet the time carelessly as they did in the golden world" (I. i. 113–14).

Here, perhaps, Shakespeare had his first experience of the hunt, recalled when he wrote of Jaques:

> . . . as he lay along
> Under an oak, whose antique root peeps out
> Upon the brook that brawls along this wood;
> To the which place a poor sequestered stag,
> That from the hunter's aim had ta'en a hurt,
> Did come to languish; and indeed, my lord,
> The wretched animal heaved forth such groans
> That their discharge did stretch his leathern coat
> Almost to bursting, and the big round tears
> Coursed one another down his innocent nose
> In piteous chase.
>
> (*As You Like It* II. i. 32–42)

FROM AN ETCHING BY MAC PHERSON IN
Land of Shakespeare.
FOLGER LIBRARY.

The Forest of Arden.

FROM BARLOW, *Various Birds.*
FOLGER LIBRARY.

Hare and hounds.

As a youth, Shakespeare would have roamed the countryside, snared birds, chased rabbits and set "springes to catch woodcocks" (*Hamlet* I. iii. 122), commonly considered the most witless of birds, therefore easily caught. All of this experience and observation found its way into the metaphors and similies of his later writing.

FROM BARLOW, *Various Birds.*
FOLGER LIBRARY.

"Springes to catch woodcocks."
(Hamlet *I. iii. 122*)

FOLGER LIBRARY.
FROM GEOFFREY WHITNEY,
A Choice of Emblems (1586).

Snaring birds in the sixteenth century.

Strolling players, who wandered about the countryside under the sponsorship of some great lord like the Earl of Leicester, came to Stratford and performed in the town hall. As bailiff, William's father gave permission for such plays, and the lad undoubtedly got his first taste for dramatic entertainment at these performances.

When he was eleven years old, a great event took place at the Earl of Leicester's castle at Kenilworth, and young William, with other active youths in the environs, may have traveled the few miles from Stratford to see the show. There the Earl of Leicester entertained Queen Elizabeth for many long days with spectacular pageantry and drama.

FROM THE TITLE PAGE OF [PAUL]
Scarron's Comical Romance (1676).
FOLGER LIBRARY.

*A group of strolling players, with a performance in
the background.*

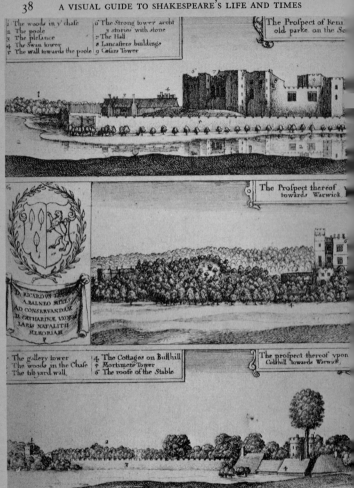

Three views of Kenilworth Castle before its destruction by Cromwell's forces in 1649.

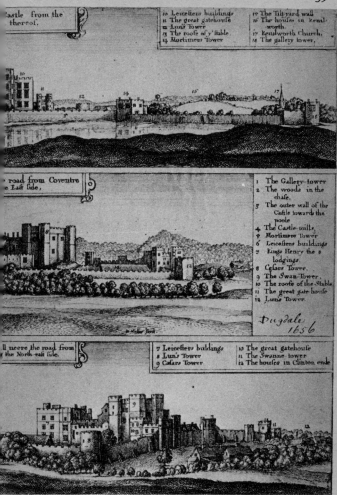

astle from the
thereof.

10 Leicesters buildings
11 The great gatehouse
12 Luns Tower
13 The roofe of y⁵ stable
14 Mortimers Tower

15 The Tilt yard wall
16 The houses in kenil-
      worth.
17 Kenilworth Church,
18 The gallery tower,

road from Coventre
e East side,

1 The Gallery-tower
2 The woods in the
      chase.
3 The outer wall of the
      Castle toward the
      poole
4 The Castle-mill,
5 Mortimers Tower
6 Leicesters buildings
7 Kings Henry the 8
      lodgings
8 Cesars Tower,
9 The Swan-tower,
10 The roofe of the stable
11 The great gate-house
12 Luns Tower

Dugdale
1656

l neere the road from
the North-east side.

7 Leicesters buldings
8 Luns Tower
9 Cesars Tower

10 The great gatehouse
11 The Swanne-tower
12 The houses in Clinton ende

FROM WILLIAM DUGDALE,
Antiquities of Warwickshire (1656).
FOLGER LIBRARY.

On an artificial lake, sham battles took place, and every day saw something staged to excite the interest of the queen and court—and of hundreds of villagers and countrymen who contrived to crowd into the palace grounds. Some years after this, in 1591 at Elvetham, the queen enjoyed a similar entertainment which Shakespeare may possibly have seen. At least he probably saw the woodcut illustration of the event which seems to be

FROM *Elvetham, an Account* (N.D.).

FOLGER LIBRARY.

The entertainment of Queen Elizabeth by the Earl of Hertford at Elvetham (1591). Note the position of the queen, "thronéd by the West."

suggested in *A Midsummer Night's Dream* (the authors have italicized the significant line):

> That very time I saw (but thou couldst not),
> Flying between the cold moon and the earth,
> Cupid, all armed. A certain aim he took
> *At a fair Vestal, thronéd by the West,*
> And loosed his love-shaft smartly from his bow,
> As it should pierce a hundred thousand hearts.

(II. i. 158–63)

As a boy growing up in Stratford, Shakespeare doubt-less heard recounted the town's great success story: the rise to wealth and fame of Sir Hugh Clopton, an earlier Stratford lad who, in the previous century, went to London, got rich as a merchant, and eventually became lord mayor of London. Sir Hugh, who died in 1492 (the year that Columbus discovered America), built the best house in Stratford, still known as New Place, and provided a stone bridge across the Avon River which even today carries the burden of all motor traffic across the river. Sir Hugh's story may have inspired the young Shakespeare to struggle for his own success in London. At any rate, when he had made enough money in London to retire, he came back to his native town and bought Sir Hugh's fine house, where he lived out his days. The original house no longer stands, but some of the foundation stones are visible in the handsome and colorful garden that still exists, planted and maintained to look as much as possible as it did in Shakespeare's time.

FROM A DRAWING BY JOHN JORDAN OF STRATFORD
(1793), SAID TO HAVE BEEN COPIED FROM A SURVEYOR'S
DRAWING OF 1590. HALLIWELL-PHILLIPPS, "ARTISTIC RECORDS."
FOLGER LIBRARY.

"A perspective view of the New Place," showing the Guild
Chapel, Guildhall and Almshouses beyond Sir Hugh Clopton's fine house.

The gardens of New Place.

As Shakespeare came to maturity, he fell in love with a girl name Anne Hathaway, who lived a short distance from Stratford—walking distance—in the hamlet of Shottery. It was, perhaps, young love remembered in the lovely setting of this cottage that later inspired Lorenzo's wooing of Jessica in *The Merchant of Venice*:

> The moon shines bright. In such a night as this,
> When the sweet wind did gently kiss the trees
> And they did make no noise—in such a night
> Troilus methinks mounted the Trojan walls
> And sighed his soul toward the Grecian tents,
> Where Cressid lay that night.
>
> (V. i. 1–6)

Although Anne was slightly older, they determined to marry, and they obtained a license on November 27, 1582. Neither the precise day nor the place of the wedding is known with certainty. Their first child, Susanna, was christened on May 26, 1583, and their other children, twins—a son Hamnet and a daughter Judith—were christened on February 2, 1585.

With a young family to provide for, Shakespeare was eager for opportunities greater than Stratford could offer. Sometime in the 1580's (the exact date is unknown), he set out from his native town for London, leaving his wife and children in Stratford.

FROM A SKETCH BY BLIGHT (1863), IN
HALLIWELL-PHILLIPPS, "ARTISTIC RECORDS."
FOLGER LIBRARY.

The interior of Anne Hathaway's cottage.

FROM DAY, *Book of Christian Prayers.*
FOLGER LIBRARY.

*A marriage ceremony in the Church of England of about
the time of Shakespeare's marriage.*

With a bundle over his shoulder, he probably walked, rather than rode, across Clopton Bridge and headed for London. The capital was the greatest city in England, indeed the only large city, and there Shakespeare would seek his fortune.

FROM A WATERCOLOR COPY OF AN EIGHTEENTH-
CENTURY PAINTING, ARTIST UNKNOWN, IN HALLIWELL-
PHILLIPPS, "ARTISTIC RECORDS."
FOLGER LIBRARY.

*A view of Clopton Bridge, looking toward the lower part of
Bridge Street. The man on horseback is headed toward
London.*

CHAPTER TWO

YOUNG
SHAKESPEARE
IN LONDON

London in Shakespeare's youth was a city of perhaps 150,000 inhabitants. It was by far the largest city in England and was the center of much activity. Ships from European ports brought their cargoes to wharves along the Thames River, London's great waterway to the sea. They loaded cargoes of wool, England's most important export, for merchants in Holland, Belgium and France. More exciting than the merchant ships from across the English Channel were vessels that brought goods from more distant ports in the Baltic and the Mediterranean seas, and from the faraway coasts of Africa and America, then beginning to be explored by Englishmen. As a German tourist said of London, "The wealth of the world is wafted to it by the Thames."

The city of London proper was the portion—still known as "the City"—that once lay behind the ancient walls built as protection against invaders. The main thoroughfares entered through heavy gates that could be shut and barred. Within a short walk outside the walls, one could still find parkland and countryside, open fields and woods.

FROM LUCAS JANSSEN WAGENAER, *The Mariners
Mirror*, TRANS. ANTHONY ASHLEY [1588].
                                    FOLGER LIBRARY.

England and the coasts of Europe.

Pieter Vanden Keere fecit 1593.

Of one of the for-
mer 12 Companies
is the Lo. Mayor
of the Cyte comonly
chosen

a. Bushops gate streete.	g. Barbican	n. Holbourn	t. Cheap syde
b. Papie	h. Aldisgate streete	s. Grayes Inn lane	u. Bucklers bu
c. Alhallowes in the wall	i. Charterhouse	y. S. Androws	w. Brodstreete
d. S. Taphins.	k. Holborne Conduit	q. Newgate	x. The stockes
e. Syluer streete.	l. Chauncery lane	r. S. Lions	y. The Exchan
f. Aldermanburyt.	m. Temple barr	s.S.Nee Shambels	z. Cornehill

The City of London.

Merchantaylors

Haberdashers

Salters

Ironmongers

Vintners

Clothworkers

Scala passuum 5 pedum
80 160 240 320 400 480

Spittle feyldes

Aldgate

Eaſt Southwarke

Olde ſwan   Bell kaye   Billinſgate   Galley kaye   Cuſtom houſe   The tower   S. Katherynes

Shruwſbury houſe

fluuius

S. Maryes
Outreys

S. Towleyes

Olde ſwan

2. Colmanſtreete   8. Fanchurche   14. Fetter lane   20. Winchester house
3. Baſſings hall   9. Marke lane   15. S Dunſhous   21. Battle bridge
4. Hunndſtetche   10. Minchyn lane   16. Thames ſtreete   22. Bermodſey ſtreete
5. Leadon hall   11. Paules   17. Ledon ſtone
6. Gratious ſtreete   12. Eaſtcheape   18. Olde Baylye   Ioannes Norden Anglus
7. Hornege houſe   13. Fleeſtreete   19. Clerkenwell   deſcripſit anno 1593

FROM JOHN NORDEN, *Speculum Britanniae* (1593).
FOLGER LIBRARY.

To the west, up the river, was another incorporated place called Westminster. This is the site of Westminster Abbey and today's Houses of Parliament, and is now a part of metropolitan London.

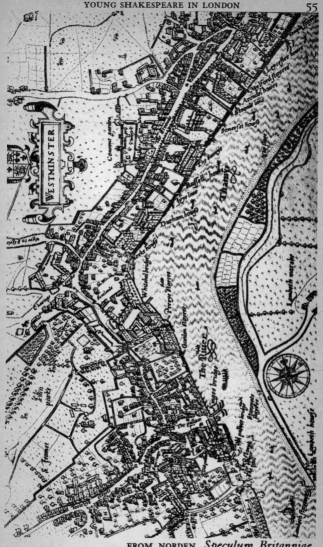

FROM NORDEN, *Speculum Britanniae.*
FOLGER LIBRARY.

A bird's-eye plan of Westminster.

Shakespeare's route from Stratford to London would have brought him along the Great West Road to Westminster. His eyes must have bulged at the sight of the great Abbey, Westminster Hall (part of old Westminster Palace), St. Stephen's Chapel (where the House of Commons then sat), St. Margaret's Church, the Palace of Whitehall and other buildings of the seat of all England's government.

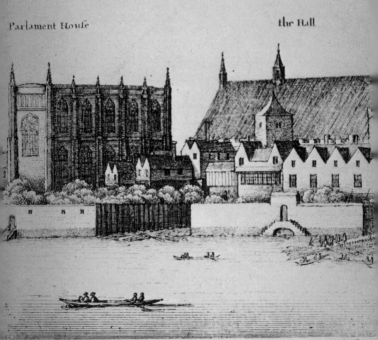

Part of the city of Westminster from the river, showing St. Stephen's Chapel (Parliament House), Westminster Hall and Westminster Abbey.

Travel in London for most people was accomplished on foot, though wealthy people might ride horses. This did not mean that traffic was not a problem. Coaches were beginning to be popular, and there were increasing complaints that congestion around the playhouses, caused by too many coaches, was acute. Tradesmen used horse-drawn carts. Ladies were sometimes carried on a "litter."

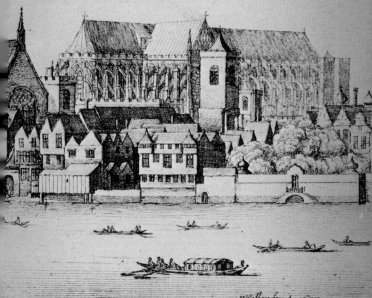

the Abby

FROM AN ENGRAVING BY WENCESLAUS HOLLAR (1647),
IN HALLIWELL-PHILLIPPS, "ARTISTIC RECORDS."
FOLGER LIBRARY.

If Shakespeare entered the City on foot through Lud-
gate, he would have made his way to the vicinity of
St. Paul's Cathedral, then a lofty Gothic building that
was burned in the Great Fire of London in 1666.
There he might have hoped to find a former Stratford

*The western part of the City, dominated by St. Paul's
Cathedral.*

neighbor, Richard Field, a printer, for printers and
booksellers populated St. Paul's Churchyard and adja-
cent streets. Field was to be the printer of Shakespeare's narrative poems, *Venus and Adonis* (1593) and
The Rape of Lucrece (1594).

FROM MATTHAEUS MERIAN, VIEW OF LONDON, FIRST
PUBLISHED IN PIERRE D'AUITY,
Neuwe archontologia cosmica (1638).
FOLGER LIBRARY.

On bookstalls in the area the young man could have picked up pamphlets and books that may have suggested themes for plays that he would write. One of the popular playwrights of the day was Christopher Marlowe; another was Thomas Kyd. Kyd's blood-and-thunder play, *A Spanish Tragedy,* may have influenced Shakespeare to imitate, in *Titus Andronicus* and even in *Hamlet,* a type of drama then exceedingly popular.

St. Paul's Cathedral from the east.

FROM AN ENGRAVING BY HOLLAR (1656?)
IN HALLIWELL- PHILLIPPS, "ARTISTIC RECORDS."
FOLGER LIBRARY.

If Shakespeare entered the City through Newgate, he would have passed Newgate Prison, from which condemned felons were dragged on sledges to the gallows at Tyburn, a site near one of the entrances to present-day Hyde Park. There they were hanged and, in the case of traitors, drawn and quartered. That is, they were disemboweled and cut into four portions.

Perfecutiones aduerfus Catholicos à Proteftanti-
bus Caluiniftis excitæ in Anglia.

Sanguinis effufi firmamus pignore Chrifti
Maiorumq̃, fidem , magni fundamina Petri,
Et tantum Latÿs apicem veneramur in oris.
At gregis electi cuftodia non cadet vnquam
In caput , ô Regina,tuum,regéſque profanos,
Et minus in vilem fidei myfteria ſexum.

L 2   MARIA

FROM [RICHARD VERSTEGAN] *Theatrum crudelitatum*
haereticorum (1592).
FOLGER LIBRARY.

Hanging, drawing and quartering.

Proceeding on through the City, he would have walked along the street known as Cheapside, looking into stalls and shops and watching people on this busy thoroughfare.

FROM A MANUSCRIPT BY HUGH ALLEY ENTITLED, "A
CAVEAT FOR THE CITY OF LONDON" (1598).
FOLGER LIBRARY.

The market in Cheapside.

Undoubtedly he would bring up at the Royal Exchange, built by a rich merchant and philanthropist named Sir Thomas Gresham. There, businessmen gathered to swap information about trade, the movement of merchant ships, the danger of war, etc. There also were hangers-on, even pickpockets and sharpers of all sorts, for sixteenth-century London was not without its crooks and rogues.

A short distance beyond the Exchange, Shakespeare would have come into Grace Church (or Gracious) Street that ran north from London Bridge. Here he was at the heart of the City, very near the Cross Keys Inn, where plays were performed and Shakespeare spent some of his early days in the theatre. Grace Church Street ran into Bishop's Gate Street and St. Helen's parish, where Shakespeare had lodgings for a time, conveniently located between the Cross Keys Inn and The Theatre and Curtain playhouses in Shoreditch, beyond Bishop's Gate in the City's north wall.

FROM HALLIWELL-PHILLIPPS,
"ADDITIONAL ARTISTIC ILLUSTRATIONS."
FOLGER LIBRARY.

The Royal Exchange of London.

FROM ALLEY, "CAVEAT." FOLGER LIBRARY.

Bishop's Gate.

ESCHEAPE : MA

FROM ALLEY, "CAVEAT." FOLGER LIBRARY.

Eastcheap Market.

Eastcheap, running east from Grace Church Street to Tower Hill, was the Elizabethan equivalent of the Left Bank of Paris or New York's Greenwich Village. Here were the taverns and lowlife that from time immemorial have lured adventurous youth. Prince Hal's progress from his roistering days in Eastcheap to the

throne in Westminster, through the two parts of Shakespeare's *Henry IV,* may chronicle to some degree the playwright's own experiences—his early delight in the rogues of Eastcheap turning gradually to disillusionment and, finally, disgust.

FROM A CONTEMPORARY WOODCUT IN THE *Roxburghe Ballads* (1866–99). FOLGER LIBRARY.

A tavern scene.

One is told in London today that the mythical Boar's Head Tavern was located at the intersection of Eastcheap and Grace Church streets. This would have put it approximately at the top of Fish Street, which led south to the wharf where fishermen unloaded their catch at Billingsgate—a name that has become a synonym for the salty language to be heard there.

FROM ALLEY, "CAVEAT." FOLGER LIBRARY.

Shakespeare's Boar's Head Tavern is thought to have been located, in his mind at least, near the intersection of Grace Church and Eastcheap. This would have placed it also near the top of Fish Street, which led from Eastcheap south to the river.

FROM ALLEY, "CAVEAT." FOLGER LIBRARY.

The fish wharf at Billingsgate.

The Thames east of London Bridge.

FROM CLAES JANSZ VISSCHER, "LONG
VIEW OF LONDON FROM THE SOUTH" (1616).
FOLGER LIBRARY.

From Billingsgate eastward Shakespeare could have made his way along the wharves where oceangoing ships loaded English wool and unloaded their cargoes of wine and leathers, silks and spices. The wharves of London were always filled with sailors telling tales of their adventures in strange parts of the world. For English sailors were daring men who found their way to most of the exciting spots in the world. From these sailors Shakespeare picked up so much information about the sea that some scholars have thought that Shakespeare must have been at one time a sailor himself.

Shakespeare's plays are nowhere more English than in the richness of their metaphors derived from the sea. In these lines from *The Merchant of Venice* he combines two images that reinforce one another.

> There where your argosies with portly sail—
> Like signiors and rich burghers on the flood,
> Or, as it were, the pageants of the sea—
> Do overpeer the petty traffickers,
> That curtsy to them, do them reverence,
> As they fly by them with their woven wings.
>
> (I. i. 9–14)

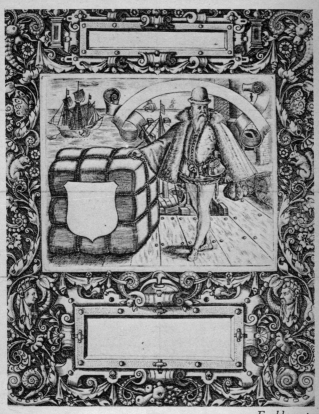

FROM THEODOR DE BRY, *Emblemata
nobilitatis* (1593).
FOLGER LIBRARY.

An English prototype for the Merchant of Venice.

If he was not for a time a sailor himself, Shakespeare observed carefully the ships he could see every day on the Thames. For example, the low "waists" of sixteenth-century vessels, where there were no rails or bulkheads for protection, inspired the vivid dream described by the Duke of Clarence in *Richard III*:

Methoughts that I had broken from the Tower,
And was embarked to cross to Burgundy,
And in my company my brother Gloucester,
Who from my cabin tempted me to walk
Upon the hatches: . . .

                   . . . As we paced along
Upon the giddy footing of the hatches,
Methought that Gloucester stumbled, and in falling
Struck me, that thought to stay him, overboard,
Into the tumbling billows of the main.

(I. iv.10–22)

FROM BARTOLOMEO CRESCENTIO,
Nautica Mediterranea (1607).
FOLGER LIBRARY.

A sixteenth-century merchantman.

Like every other newcomer to the City, Shakespeare, of course, visited the Tower of London, the huge castle, begun by William the Conqueror, which straddled the eastern wall of the City. Though it had other uses, the Tower, a gloomy pile of buildings, heavily battlemented, was always associated with its prison and

The Tower of London.

many tragic stories circulated about it to stimulate a
writer's imagination. If Shakespeare approached the
Tower by boat, he would have seen Traitor's Gate,
pictured here, through which condemned prisoners
were often taken to the dungeons.

the TOWER

FROM AN ENGRAVING BY HOLLAR (CA. 1647), IN
AN EXTRA-ILLUSTRATED COPY OF ARTHUR WILSON,
History of Great Britain (1653).
FOLGER LIBRARY.

Returning westward on the Thames, Shakespeare could have passed under London Bridge. On the bridge above him shopkeepers plied their trades in stalls and half-timbered houses. On the south end of the bridge, however, Shakespeare, as other travelers, might have been horrified to see the moldering heads of traitors stuck on pikes high atop the Southwark Gate.

FROM VISSCHER, "LONG VIEW OF LONDON."
FOLGER LIBRARY.

London Bridge. "Shooting the Bridge" was hazardous and could only be undertaken at certain times of the tide. If the tide were not right, commuters left their water taxis on one side of the bridge, crossed on foot, and hired another boat on the opposite side.

FROM MERIAN'S VIEW OF LONDON. FOLGER LIBRARY.

The Southwark Gate of London Bridge.

For those who could afford it, the Thames provided
an easy means of transportation up and down the populated areas that lined its banks. To get about, one could
hire a water taxi, a small boat called a wherry. River
travel was much employed by the great noblemen who

The palace at Greenwich, called Placentia.

had fine houses with gardens running down to the river. Some of the queen's palaces were also situated on the river. She herself liked to travel from one palace to another in her resplendent royal barge.

FROM AN ENGRAVING DATED APRIL 23, 1767, IN
HALLIWELL-PHILLIPPS, "ARTISTIC RECORDS."
FOLGER LIBRARY.

Across the Thames was a region called the Bankside. In this area the City authorities exercised no control and there in time grew up various theatres and pleasure resorts. It was here that Shakespeare's theatrical company would erect a theatre called the Globe.

When Shakespeare reached London, sometime in the 1580's, there was much talk of war with Spain. English ship captains encountered Spanish treasure ships on the high seas and captured them. English volunteers were going across the North Sea to Holland to enlist in the Dutch armies fighting for independence from Spain. By 1588 open war had broken out with Spain. The English in the summer of that year managed to defeat the great Spanish Armada. In any case, London all during the 1580's and early '90's was an exciting place for any young man with curiosity and imagination.

At some time in the late 1580's, Shakespeare must have seen the great *Ark Royal,* flagship of the lord admiral at the Armada battle. Perhaps the first time was soon after the victory of 1588, with all her sails set and pennants flying, splendid with exhilaration that carried over into Romeo's lines of high expectation:

And bring thee cords made like a tackled stair,
Which to the high topgallant of my joy
Must be my convoy in the secret night.

(*Romeo and Juliet* II. iv. 183–85)

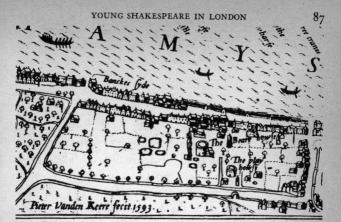

FROM NORDEN, *Speculum Britanniae.*

FOLGER LIBRARY.

The Bankside in 1593, showing the Bear Garden or "Beare howse," and the Rose, an early playhouse in the area.

The Ark Royal, flagship of the English fleet that defeated the Spanish Armada, was one of the few English galleons of the time rigged with topgallant sails—the third sail up the mast.

FROM JOHN CHARNOCK, *History of Marine Architecture* (1801).

FOLGER LIBRARY.

Accounts of the Armada battle were published and told in countless versions by participants. The climax of the long-running fight up the Channel came when the lord admiral, taking advantage of wind and tide, released fireships into the midst of the Spanish fleet off Calais, the operation that is pictured here. Although Shakespeare's *Henry V* concerns a land war in another time (he wisely never wrote about current events), the patriotism that pervades the play mirrors the temper of the time of the Armada.

We do not know where Shakespeare found a room on arrival, but it may have been with friends of the family, or in some lodging house. At night, along the darkened streets, he would have watched the bellman with his lantern who served as watchman, calling the hours and announcing that all was well. This same bellman also went through the streets to announce a death. In these lines from *Macbeth* Shakespeare was to combine both functions:

It was the owl that shrieked, the fatal bellman
Which gives the stern'st good-night.

(II. ii. 5–6)

*The Armada battle took place in the English Channel in the
summer of 1588.*

A London bellman.

Death in Shakespeare's time was often the occasion
of much pomp and ceremony. The death of a sovereign meant long processions, as indeed it does today.
But the death of a great nobleman like Sir Philip
Sidney, a young hero killed fighting for Dutch independence in 1586, was also the occasion of a cere-
monial march through London, part of which—the
hearse—is depicted in the drawing shown here. The
funeral pomp often worked into Shakespeare's plays—

FROM THOMAS
LANT, *Sequitur
celebritas
et pompa
funeris* (1587).
FOLGER LIBRARY.

*The funeral
cortege of Sir
Philip Sidney.*

Ophelia's burial, for example, and the famous wooing scene before the coffin of Henry VI in *Richard III*—took their pageantry from the streets of London:

> Set down, set down your honorable load—
> If honor may be shrouded in a hearse—
> Whilst I awhile obsequiously lament
> The untimely fall of virtuous Lancaster.

> (I. ii. 1–4)

The star of all of London's pageantry was the queen herself. She was frequently to be seen going in state to the opening of Parliament, or setting out on a summer progress, or attending a marriage of the nobility, as pictured here. When Elizabeth went in procession, a great body of her nobles surrounded her, led by the lord chamberlain, the man who was the patron and protector of the dramatic company that Shakespeare eventually joined.

FROM AN ANONYMOUS
ENGRAVING.
FOLGER LIBRARY.

Queen Elizabeth I in procession to a wedding of nobility in Blackfriars.

Whatever Shakespeare did on arrival in London, we can be certain that he kept his eyes and ears open to the sights and sounds of the city, the ships that came and went, the talk and gossip about the docks and taverns, passing comment in the streets, and, above all, the pageantry that was characteristic of Elizabethan England—the stuff of which drama is made.

CHAPTER THREE

SHAKESPEARE'S
THEATRE

When Shakespeare came to London to make his name as a player and playwright, the status of actors was low. They were classified by law as vagrants, which were listed as "rogues, vagabonds, common players, and sturdy beggars." Plays themselves were not considered "literature" and had about the status of many television scripts today. Yet Shakespeare brought dignity to the profession of acting and elevated plays to the highest form of literary production. He himself, however, wrote his sonnets and narrative poems in order to be regarded as a man of letters.

Because players, particularly when they went traveling in the provinces, needed the support of a great patron to keep from running afoul of the law as vagrants, they sought and received the protection of some

FROM THOMAS HARMAN,
*A Caveat or Warning for
Common Cursetors* (1567).
FOLGER LIBRARY.

*A vagrant, or beggar, with
whom Elizabethan actors were
frequently classed.*

[Lord Hunsdon.]

FROM AN ANONYMOUS
ENGRAVING. FOLGER LIBRARY.

*George Carey, second Lord
Hunsdon, who succeeded his
father (1597) as lord chamberlain and patron of Shakespeare's company.*

nobleman. Shakespeare joined the players whose patron
was Lord Hunsdon, later the lord chamberlain. They
became known as Lord Hunsdon's Men. When Huns-

Euery
MAN IN
HIS
HVMOVR.

A Comœdie.

Acted in the yeere 1598. By the then
Lord Chamberlaine his
Seruants.

The Author B. I.

I U V E N.

Haud tamen inuide.a vati, quem pulpita pascunt.

LONDON,

Printed by WILLIAM STANSBY.

M. DC. XVI.

*Title page of a popular play of Ben Jonson
performed by the Lord Chamberlain's Men
in 1598.*

don was elevated to lord chamberlain, they became the
Lord Chamberlain's Men, or, as listed here, "the Lord
Chamberlain his Servants."

---

(72)

This Comoedie was firſt
Acted, in the yeere
1598.

By the then L. CHAMBERLAYNE
bis Seruants.

The principall Comœdians were.

WILL SHAKESPEARE.	RIC. BVRBADGE.
AVG. PHILIPS.	IOH. HEMINGS.
HEN. CONDEL.	THO. POPE.
WILL. SLYE.	CHR. BEESTON.
WILL. KEMPE.	IOH. DVKE.

With the allowance of the Maſter of REVELLS.

FOLGER LIBRARY.

The list of players from Ben Jonson's Every
Man in His Humor. *Published in 1616,
this edition lists Shakespeare first.*

When James I became king of England in 1603, Shakespeare's company went under the protection of the sovereign himself and was thereafter known as "the King's Men."

FROM WILSON, *History of Great Britain.*
FOLGER LIBRARY.

King James I, patron of the King's Men.

Shakespeare's group, though important, was not the only company of players. A significant rival was the Lord Admiral's Men, managed by a half-literate genius named Philip Henslowe, who kept a very important

FROM WILSON, *History*, FOLGER LIBRARY.

Charles Howard, lord admiral of England, victor over the Spanish Armada and patron of the Lord Admiral's Men. Like the lord chamberlain, he was an influential member of the Queen's Privy Council.

account book showing his payments to playwrights and actors. This book has survived and is known as *Henslowe's Diary*.

layd owt for my lord admeralles meane as foloweth 1597   **F. 44**
1597

pd vnto antony monday & drayton for the laste
payment of the Boocke of mother Readcape the } lv^s   5
5 of Jenewary 1597 the some of . . . .

Layd [of] for cop^r lace ∧ & for a valle for the boye a } xxix^s
geanste the playe of dido & enevs the 3 of Jeneway 1597

Lent vnto thomas dowton the 8 of Jeneway 1597 } xx^s
twentyshillinges to by a boockes of m^r dickers lent   10

Lent vnto the company when they fyrst played
dido at nyght the some of thritishillynges } xxx^s
wch wasse the 8 of Jeneway 1597 J saye . . . . .

lent vnto the company the 15 of Jeneway 1597
to bye a boocke of m^r dicker called fayeton } iiij^ll   15
fower pownde   J saye lent . . . .

lent vnto Thomas dowton for the company
to paye to the m^r of the Revells for lysensynge of } ix^s
ij boockes xiiij^s a bated to dowton v^s so Reaste

lent vnto Thomas dowton for the company
to bye a sewte for phayeton & ij Rebates } iij^ll   20
& j fardengalle the 26 of Jeneway 1598 the
some of three pownde   J saye lent . . . . .

lent vnto Thomas dowton the 28 of Jeneway
1598 to bye a whitte satten dublette for } xxxx^s   25
phayeton fortyshyllenges   J saye lent . . . . .

lent vnto the companey the 4 of febreary
1598 to dise charge m^r dicker owt of the } xxxx^s
cownter in the powltrey the some of fortie
shillinges J saye dd to thomas dowton . . .

Layd owt vnto antony monday the 15 of febreary   30
1598 for a playe boocke called the firste parte of } v^ll
Robyne hoode . . . .

83

A page from Henslowe's Diary *as reproduced in the edition by W. W. Greg (1904).*

Henslowe's son-in-law was Edward Alleyn, an important player and actor-manager. He was the first to play the title role of Christopher Marlowe's *Doctor*

FROM AN ENGRAVING AFTER THE
PORTRAIT AT DULWICH COLLEGE.
FOLGER LIBRARY.

Edward Alleyn, star of the Lord Admiral's company.

Faustus. In the scene where he is supposed to call up seven devils, during a performance at Exeter, he was terrified to see *eight* devils and believed the real Devil had appeared with the make-believe ones. He vowed to found the College of God's Gift at Dulwich if he got

The Tragicall Historie of the Life and Death of Doctor Faustus.

With new Additions.

Written by CH. MAR.

Printed at London for *Iohn Wright*, and are to be sold at his shop without Newgate. 1631.

One of the devils coming up through a trapdoor in a scene from Marlowe's Doctor Faustus, *as illustrated on the title page of his play (1631 ed.).*

back to London alive. And thus was founded an institution that exists to this day in London.

We do not know when Shakespeare joined the Lord Chamberlain's Men, but we do know that he was a member and part owner of the company when it

The Workes of William Shakespeare,

containing all his Comedies, Histories, and Tragedies: Truely set forth, according to their first *ORIGINALL.*

The Names of the Principall Actors
in all these Playes.

William Shakespeare.	Samuel Gilburne.
Richard Burbadge.	Robert Armin.
John Hemmings.	William Ostler.
Augustine Phillips.	Nathan Field.
William Kempt.	John Underwood.
Thomas Poope.	Nicholas Tooley.
George Bryan.	William Ecclestone.
Henry Condell.	Joseph Taylor.
William Slye.	Robert Benfield.
Richard Cowly.	Robert Goughe.
John Lowine.	Richard Robinson.
Samuell Crosse.	Iohn Shancke.
Alexander Cooke.	Iohn Rice.

FOLGER LIBRARY.

The King's Men as listed in the First Folio edition of Shakespeare's plays (1623). This copy is autographed by one of the players, Samuel Gilburne.

erected the famous Globe Theatre in 1598. The list of players in the First Folio edition of Shakespeare's plays (1623) includes the following: Richard Burbage, who first played Hamlet and other great tragic roles; Will Kemp, the original Dogberry of *Much Ado About Nothing* and Bottom of *A Midsummer Night's Dream;*

FROM AN ENGRAVING AFTER THE
PORTRAIT AT DULWICH COLLEGE.
FOLGER LIBRARY.

Richard Burbage, the first Hamlet.

FROM AN ANONYMOUS ENGRAVING. FOLGER LIBRARY.

*Will Kemp made a wager that he could dance from London
to Norwich, a distance of 100 miles. He is shown here performing that stunt.*

Robert Armin, for whom Shakespeare wrote such parts as Feste in *Twelfth Night* and the Fool in *King Lear;* John Lowin, one of the last players to join the company; and, of course, William Shakespeare.

FROM THE TITLE PAGE OF ARMIN'S *Two Maids of More-clacke* (1609).
FOLGER LIBRARY.

Robert Armin succeeded Kemp as chief clown in Shakespeare's company. Armin's specialty was singing rather than dancing, and for his special talents Shakespeare wrote such parts as Feste in Twelfth Night *and the Fool in* King Lear.

FROM AN ENGRAVING AFTER
THE PORTRAIT IN THE
ASHMOLEAN MUSEUM, OXFORD.
FOLGER LIBRARY.

John Lowin, who joined the company later and lived longer than most of the other players.

FOLGER LIBRARY.

This drawing by Ozias Humphrey (1783) is a sketch copy of the so-called Chandos portrait of Shakespeare. There is an unproved tradition that the original was painted by Shakespeare's friend and colleague, Richard Burbage.

Elizabethan actors were versatile and talented. They had to be able to play a variety of parts including women. (There were no actresses at this time.) Many of the plays depended for their effects on the ability of the actors to fence, to dance, even to sing. These were activities that the populace as a whole engaged in, so the audiences were critical.

Giacomo Di Grassi, His True Art of Defence (1594).
FOLGER LIBRARY.

A lesson in fencing with sword and shield from a contemporary fencing manual.

Elizabethan audiences relished comic scenes of clownery, which explains many of the comic subplots in Shakespeare's plays, among which were the Falstaff scenes. Before Will Kemp and Robert Armin, Richard Tarleton had been so famous as a clown that he annoyed playwrights by interpolating his own lines in his performances, a trick of other famous clowns. In *Hamlet,* Shakespeare took occasion to put into the prince's mouth his opinion of this sort of clownish performance:

And let those that play your clowns speak no more than is set down for them. For there be of them that will themselves laugh, to set on some quantity of barren spectators to laugh too, though in the meantime some necessary question of the play be then to be considered. That's villainous and shows a most pitiful ambition in the fool that uses it.

(III. ii. 37–43)

RICHARD TARLETON
one of the first Actors in
SHAKESPEARS PLAYS.

A contemporary woodcut showing Richard Tarleton, the famous clown who sometimes interpolated his own lines into Shakespeare's plays.

English players in Shakespeare's time frequently went on tour, and sometimes made tours to the continent of Europe. Their clownery particularly entertained foreign audiences. Will Kemp, for example, was a member of a troupe that played at Elsinore, in Denmark, a fact that may have made Shakespeare aware of this site. Kemp may have described to him the setting he used so vividly for *Hamlet*.

By the time that Shakespeare retired from the theatre and returned to Stratford, the acting profession had acquired a new dignity; later ages were to say that the art of drama had been raised to the level of its highest achievements.

Shakespear y Player by Garter

FROM AN ANONYMOUS MANUSCRIPT (CA. 1600).
FOLGER LIBRARY.

A rough sketch of Shakespeare's coat of arms, identifying him as a player.

A contemporary view of Elsinore, Denmark, as it was when Will Kemp played there.

FROM BRAUN AND HOGENBERG, *Civitates orbis terrarum*
(1572–1618). COURTESY, THE HENRY E. HUNTINGTON
LIBRARY AND ART GALLERY.

Players came before playhouses. Plays at first were given in the halls of the nobility, town halls, even churches (for Christmas and Easter plays), inns, and the courtyards of inns. One of these, the George, still exists in London. The shape of the innyard, where the

FROM AN ANONYMOUS ENGRAVING. FOLGER LIBRARY.

The courtyard of a Southwark inn, typical of the innyards that were used for plays.

actors set up their movable stage at one end, and where the gentry sat around the balconies and others stood in the open courtyard, influenced the shape and conditions of the first open-air theatres.

FROM A PHOTOGRAPH. FOLGER LIBRARY.

The theatre of the Folger Shakespeare Library, Washington, D. C., built to represent a characteristic Shakespearean playhouse. The seats in the "yard" and canopied ceiling are concessions to modern comfort.

The earliest playhouses on the City side of the
Thames were The Theatre and the Curtain. In these,
Shakespeare probably got his first chance in the theatre.
The city aldermen of London were suspicious of players
and playhouses because they lured young workers, the

MAP OF LONDON SHOWING THE PLAYHOUSES

BLACKFRIARS. (FIRST) 1576 -1584.
BLACKFRIARS.(SECOND) 1596 -1655.
CURTAIN. 1577 - after 1627.
FORTUNE. (FIRST) 1600- 1621.
FORTUNE. (SECOND) 1623-1661.
GLOBE. (FIRST) 1599 - 1613.
GLOBE. (SECOND) 1614 -1645.
HOPE. 1613 - after 1682.
PHOENIX or COCKPIT. 1017 - after 1664.
RED BULL. about 1605 - after 1663.
ROSE. 1587 - 1605.
SALISBURY COURT. 1629 -1666.
SWAN. 1595 - after 1632.
THEATRE. 1576 - 1598.
WHITEFRIARS. about 1605 -1614 (?).

*The theatre district of Shakespeare's London: a modern
rendering based upon contemporary maps. The Hope playhouse here replaced the Bear Garden in 1613.*

apprentices, from their jobs and tended to cause dis-
order and unruliness. Hence the theatres tried to locate
in areas outside the jurisdiction of the aldermen, such
as Shoreditch beyond the City Wall, through Bishop's
Gate.

FROM J. Q. ADAMS, *Shakespearean Playhouses* (1917).
                                                FOLGER LIBRARY.

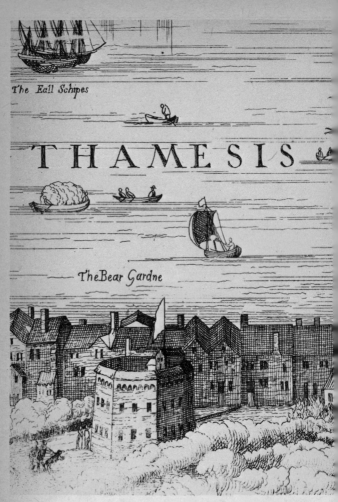

The Eall Schipes

THAMESIS

TheBear Gardne

The Bear Garden and the Globe.

The Gally fufte

The Globe

FROM VISSCHER, "LONG VIEW OF LONDON."
FOLGER LIBRARY.

Another place where players could be free from inter-
ference by the London authorities was a park area
across London Bridge from the City on what was
known as the Bankside. Already this area was known
for bear- and bull-baiting in an amphitheatre called
the Bear Garden. Here, too, Henslowe's company had
occupied the two theatres called the Rose and the Swan.

In December of 1598, Shakespeare's company dis-
mantled The Theatre in Shoreditch, moved the timbers
across the river and built the Globe, most famous of
all Elizabethan playhouses.

Exterior construction of the Globe as represented in a model built by John Cranford Adams and Irwin Smith.

We do not have blueprints of any Elizabethan play-houses, and scholars do not all agree about details of their construction. We know the Fortune playhouse was rectangular, for some of the details of the contract for its construction have survived. We believe that the Globe was circular inside and either circular or octagonal on the outside. Some exterior pictures show one form and some another.

FOLGER LIBRARY.

*Main entrance of the Globe, as represented in the Adams-
Smith model. The sign with Hercules holding the world on
his shoulders is conjectural, based upon several clues found
in contemporary writings.*

The stage was a bare platform jutting out into the audience without a curtain at the forefront. (There were curtains to conceal the inner stage.)

A trapdoor, or perhaps several traps, could let ghosts and devils (as in *Hamlet* and Marlowe's *Faustus*) come up from purgatory or hell.

*Interior of the Swan playhouse, as sketched by Arend van
Buchel from a description by his friend Johannes De Witt,
a German traveler who visited the Swan in 1596.*

An inner stage on the main level, and perhaps on upper levels, could be curtained off or used for cave and bedroom scenes. Balconies above the doors on the main stage could be used for such scenes as the balcony scene in *Romeo and Juliet*. An upper stage in the rear could also be used for scenes like Cleopatra's monument in *Antony and Cleopatra*.

A view of the various levels of the stage in the Adams-Smith model of the Globe.

A canopylike structure over the stage was called "the heavens"; from it, angels or gods might descend from a trap in the floor above.

FOLGER LIBRARY.

A view of the upper stage and "heavens" in the Adams-Smith model of the Globe.

Above "the heavens" was a room where the actors could change their costumes which was called the "tiring house."

FOLGER LIBRARY.

The "tiring house" above the apron stage of the Adams-Smith model.

(264)

CXXX.

Ludus Scenicus.

A Stage-Play.

In

FROM JOHANN A. COMENIUS,
Orbis sensualium pictus (1685).
FOLGER LIBRARY.

A scene from a play showing "groundlings" standing in the

(265)

In a Play-house, 1.	In *Theatro*, 1.
which is trimmed with Hangings, 2.	(quod vestitur *Tapetibus*, 2.
and covered with Curtains, 3.	& *Sipariis* 3.
Comedies,	tegitur)
and Tragedies	aguntur *Comœdiæ*
are acted,	vel *Tragœdiæ*,
wherein memorable	quibus repræsentantur
things are represented;	res memorabiles;
as here,	ut hic,
the History	Historia
of the Prodigal Son, 4.	de *Filio prodigo*, 4.
and his Father, 5.	& *Patre*, 5. ipsius,
by whom	a quo
he is entertained,	recipitur,
being returned home.	domum redux.
The Players	*Actores* (*histriones*)
act	agunt
being in disguise;	personati;
the Fool, 6.	*Morio*, 6.
maketh Jests.	dat Jocos.
The chief of the Spectators sit in the Gallery, 7.	Spectatorum primarii, sedent in *Orchestra*; 7.
the common sort stand on the Ground, 8.	Plebs stat in *Cavea*, 8.
and clap the hands if any thing please them.	& plaudit, si quid arridet.

Præstigiæ.

yard watching the performance. This illustration is of somewhat later date and is continental rather than English in
origin. Shakespeare's stage did not have a front curtain like
the one shown here, but in other respects was similar.

Theatres like the Globe, Rose, Swan, etc., were called "public playhouses." They were amphitheatres, looking somewhat like a stadium. The balconies and stage were the only covered portions. The customers in the "yard," later to become the "pit" of modern theatres, had to take the weather and were called "groundlings." Plays in the public playhouses took place in the afternoon, weather permitting. A flag flying over the theatre indicated that a play would be given that day.

A few playhouses were built in enclosed areas with roofs over the whole. These were called "private playhouses," but that simply meant that they played to somewhat more restricted audiences who could afford to pay a slightly higher fee. Anyone with the price could get in. Plays were given in the private playhouses at night by candlelight.

The best known of the private playhouses was the Blackfriars, on the site of the present London Times Building. It occupied a large room in the old, and then-ruinous, Blackfriars Monastery, which had been taken over earlier for various secular activities. Shakespeare's company acquired the lease to this indoor theatre in 1608 and began to use it for their own performances, probably in 1609 or 1610.

Changling   Simpleton

Sr I Falstafe   Hostes   Clause

French Dancing Mr

FROM FRANCIS KIRKMAN, *The Wits* (1662).
FOLGER LIBRARY.

*Popular stage characters of the time, including Shakespeare's
Falstaff and Hostess, shown on the stage of a "private"
theatre lighted by candlelight.*

The deed given to Shakespeare for property that he acquired in the Blackfriars. It is one of the few

surviving documents that Shakespeare actually held in his hands. The "consideration" was £140.

In 1613 Shakespeare bought property of his own in Blackfriars precinct, not far from the theatre. It is thought that the house he bought was for investment rather than for his own use, as shortly thereafter he retired to Stratford. This acquisition of property, in London as well as in Stratford, is an indication of the success and growing prosperity of Shakespeare and the King's Men.

FROM AN ORIGINAL
DRAWING BY BLIGHT (1867),
IN HALLIWELL-PHILLIPPS,
"ARTISTIC RECORDS."
FOLGER LIBRARY.

*The great hall of Middle Temple,
one of the Inns-of-Court, where*
Twelfth Night *was performed
on February 2, 1602.*

Plays were sometimes given at the Inns-of-Court, the inns where young lawyers received their training and where many older lawyers dined or had their quarters. *A Comedy of Errors*, probably Shakespeare's *The Comedy of Errors*, was performed at Gray's Inn on December 28, 1594, and *Twelfth Night* was performed at the Middle Temple on February 2, 1602.

Plays were acted in the halls of the nobility on great occasions. *A Midsummer Night's Dream* is believed to have been performed at some noble wedding celebration.

Finally, plays were often commanded to be performed before the sovereigns in one of the royal palaces. Both Queen Elizabeth and King James loved plays and delighted in having Shakespeare's company perform at court. Many of his plays were thus acted before one or the other of the sovereigns.

Queen Elizabeth is said to have liked Falstaff so much in *Henry IV* that she commanded Shakespeare to write a play showing the old scoundrel in love, with the result that *The Merry Wives of Windsor* was written and performed at court. *Macbeth* had in it an obvious tribute to King James and was also performed before that sovereign.

The first Globe Theatre burned down in 1613 during a performance of *Henry VIII* from wadding in a gun fired as a royal salute at the entrance of the player king. Contemporary accounts of the event provide clues to the construction of the theatre:

Upon St. Peter's Day Last, the playhouse or theatre called the Globe, upon the Bankside, near London, by negligent discharge of a peal of ordnance, close to the south side thereof, the thatch took fire, and the wind suddenly dispersed the flames round about, and in a very short space the whole build-

FROM A WATERCOLOR BY RICHARD HAMILTON
ESSEX (1802–55).
FOLGER LIBRARY.

Interior view of Crosby Hall, which once stood in Bishops-
gate and at one time was the residence of the Duke of
Gloucester (later Richard III). The picture represents an
imagined entry of players to perform in the great hall.

ing was quite consumed; and no man hurt: the house being filled with people to behold the play, *viz.* of Henry the Eight.

(Stow's *Annals* (1631), p. 1003)

A letter written by Sir Henry Wotton adds: "yet nothing did perish but wood and straw, and a few forsaken cloaks." Ben Jonson left the most famous ac-

FROM AN ENGRAVING AFTER HOLLAR IN JOHN SELLER,
A Book of the Prospects . . . of London (ca. 1700).
FOLGER LIBRARY.

Whitehall from the river in King James's time. The tall building at center rear is the Banqueting House designed by Inigo Jones, the only building of Whitehall Palace that survives today. Next to it was the Tudor Great Hall. Many plays were performed at Whitehall.

count of the disaster in his *Execration Against Vulcan* (1640):

> The Globe, the glory of the Bank,
> Which, though it were the fort of the whole parish,
> Flanked with a ditch, and forced out of a marish,
> I saw with two poor chambers taken in,
> And razed ere thought could urge this might have been!
> See the world's ruins! nothing but the piles
> Left—and wit since to cover it with tiles.

So we know that the new Globe was roofed with tiles instead of thatch and that the first Globe—Shakespeare's Globe—was recognized in its time, as ever since, as "the glory of the Bank."

FROM HOLLAR'S VIEW OF LONDON (1647).
FOLGER LIBRARY.

A view of the second Globe, mislabeled "Beere bayting." The engraver apparently switched labels and placed the name of the Globe on the Bear Garden.

CHAPTER FOUR

ELIZABETH I
AND JAMES I

The London of Shakespeare's mature years was the teeming center of English life. Everything had its focus in London. The queen held court there and all England kept its eyes on the doings of the sovereign. London was also the largest city in England, the chief port and the greatest place of trade in the kingdom. Sooner or later everyone of importance came to London. For amusement, visitors and residents alike found entertainment in the playhouses where Shakespeare had found a place and was making a success as an actor, as a playwright and as a member of a company of players.

When Shakespeare arrived in London in the late 1580's, the queen had been on the throne for the average lifetime of an Elizabethan, which in this period was only about thirty years. In the year 1588, perhaps the very year that Shakespeare reached London, all England was excited and concerned over the danger of a Spanish invasion, for King Philip II had sent his "Invincible" Armada against England in the summer of that year. Queen Elizabeth herself had gone to Tilbury down the Thames to review the troops and had declared that she was ready to give her blood, if necessary, in defense of her country:

I am come amongst you . . . at this time, not for my recreation and disport, but being resolved, in the midst and heat of the battle, to live or die amongst you all, to lay down for my God, and for my kingdom, and for my people, my honor and

FROM AN ENGRAVING AFTER THE PORTRAIT ATTRIBUTED TO
WILLIAM SEGAR [1585] AT HATFIELD HOUSE.
FOLGER LIBRARY.

*The "Ermine Portrait" of Queen Elizabeth as she was about
the time of the Armada.*

my blood, even in the dust. I know I have the
body of a weak and feeble woman, but I have the
heart and stomach of a king—and of a King of
England too!

The English king that this speech would have brought
to English minds was Henry V, hero of Agincourt in
the days when France, not Spain, was the great enemy.
In the decade of the Spanish war, following the
Armada, plays on English history were popular and
reflected the patriotic fervor that the continuing Spanish threat had aroused. Shakespeare's *Henry V* is perhaps the best example of this type. Like Elizabeth at
Tilbury, the king goes among his troops before the
battle, rousing their spirits with a speech that has been
quoted to British troops in every military crisis since:

> O, do not wish one more!
> Rather proclaim it, Westmoreland, through my host,
> That he which hath no stomach to this fight,
> Let him depart; his passport shall be made, . . .
> This day is called the Feast of Crispian.
> He that outlives this day, and comes safe home,
> Will stand a-tiptoe when this day is named
> And rouse him at the name of Crispian.

> (IV. iii. 37–47)

Henry V rouses the spirits of his troops in a scene from an Old Vic production of the play.

At Tilbury, Queen Elizabeth was accompanied by some of her trusted courtiers, including her favorite, the Earl of Leicester. Leicester had been the English commander in Holland when the Dutch fought for their independence from Spain. In 1588 Leicester was in command of English land forces marshaled for defense against a Spanish invasion. Soon afterward Leicester died of a sudden illness, a few days after he had written the queen to ask after her own health, "the chiefest thing in this world" to him. On the outside fold of this letter the queen wrote "His Last Letter" and put it away among her personal effects, where it was found after her own death.

Queen Elizabeth surrounded herself with able men. One was her cousin, Charles Howard, Earl of Nottingham, the lord admiral who had given her victory over the Spanish Armada.

The right nonourble and noble Lord Robert Dudley Earle of Leicester Baron of Denbigh Knight of the noble Ordres of St George and St Michael Mr of the horse to Queene ELIZABETH high Steward of her Houshold and of her Privy Counsell Lord Governour and Captaine Generall of the United Provinces in Netherland ere He deceassed in Septembr Anº 1588 and lieth Honourably entombed at Warwick by the Right noble and Vertuous Lady LETICE Countesse of Leicester unto whome this Portraicture is humbly consecrated.

Are to be sould by Comp Holland
over against the Exchange.

Ro Vaughan Sculp.

FROM HUMPHREY DYSON,
A Book Containing Proclamations (1618).
FOLGER LIBRARY.

Robert Dudley, Earl of Leicester, who entertained the queen so lavishly at Kenilworth in 1575, was commanding general of the English forces fighting with the Dutch against Spain in 1586. This portrait shows him in that role; a battle in the Low Countries is shown in the background.

Perhaps her most trusted adviser was a prudent, cautious man: William Cecil, Lord Burghley. It has been supposed that Shakespeare had him in mind when he wrote the lines on Polonius's advice to his son, Laertes, in *Hamlet*:

And these few precepts in thy memory
Look thou character. . . .
Those friends thou hast, and their adoption tried,
Grapple them to thy soul with hoops of steel;
But do not dull thy palm with entertainment
Of each new-hatched, unfledged comrade . . .
Neither a borrower nor a lender be;
For loan oft loses both itself and friend,
And borrowing dulls the edge of husbandry.

(I. iii. 62–81)

Sometime in the early 1580's Burghley had written for his son Robert (later to succeed him as chief adviser in the Privy Council) a set of instructions entitled *Certain Precepts for the Well Ordering of a Man's Life*. These precepts were printed in 1617, but they circulated in manuscript copies in Burghley's lifetime and it is possible that Shakespeare saw or heard of them. Among the precepts were these:

Let thy kindred and allies be welcome to thy table, grace them with thy countenance, and ever further them in all honest actions, for by that means thou

FROM AN ENGRAVING IN WILSON, *History of Great Britain*.
FOLGER LIBRARY.

*William Cecil, Lord Burghley, in the robes of a knight of
the garter.*

shalt . . . double the bond of nature. . . . But shake off these glowworms . . . who will feed and fawn upon thee in the summer of prosperity, but in any adverse storm they will shelter thee no more than an arbor in winter. . . .

Neither borrow money of a neighbor or friend but rather from a mere stranger, where paying for it thou mayest hear no more of it, for otherwise thou shalt eclipse thy credit, lose thy freedom, and yet pay to him as dear as to the other.

(Reprinted in *Advice to a Son,*
edited by Louis B. Wright, 1962)

Queen Elizabeth also liked to have brilliant young men in her court. One of these was Walter Raleigh, who had attempted to found a colony in the New World, and had named the land Virginia in honor of the Virgin Queen.

FROM AN ENGRAVING AFTER THE PORTRAIT IN THE
NATIONAL PORTRAIT GALLERY, LONDON, IN T. F.
HENDERSON, *James I and VI* (1904).
FOLGER LIBRARY.

*Sir Walter Raleigh, courtier, scholar and adventurer, who
founded the Roanoke Colony and named the whole territory
Virginia for the Virgin Queen.*

Another dashing—and spoiled—young courtier was the Earl of Essex, who later attempted a rebellion against the queen. The night before his followers rose in revolt, they engaged Shakespeare's company to perform *Richard II* at Essex House in London, a play that shows the deposition of a sovereign. Queen Elizabeth declared afterward that she knew she was being equated with the deposed monarch. "I am Richard II," she said to the historian William Lambarde, "know ye not that? . . . This tragedy [of *Richard II*] was played forty times in open streets and houses." Elizabeth was, in fact, not in the least like Shakespeare's characterization of Richard—which probably explains why, in her case, the attempt failed. It was Essex who lost his head.

FROM AN ENGRAVING AFTER A PORTRAIT
BY NICHOLAS HILLIARD.
FOLGER LIBRARY.

Robert Devereux, Earl of Essex, stepson of the Earl of Leicester.

The admiration and adulation of Englishmen, especially that of the poets, made a cult of the queen. Everybody talked about what was going on at court. Edmund Spenser wrote *The Faerie Queene,* the very title of which was a tribute to Elizabeth. Though she was growing old when Shakespeare was winning his greatest laurels in the playhouse, her splendor was undiminished, as indicated in his reference to her in *A Midsummer Night's Dream*:

> A certain aim he took
> At a fair Vestal, thronéd by the West,
> And loosed his love-shaft smartly from his bow,
> As it should pierce a hundred thousand hearts.
> But I might see young Cupid's fiery shaft
> Quenched in the chaste beams of the wat'ry moon,*
> And the imperial vot'ress passed on,
> In maiden meditation, fancy-free.

(II. i. 160–67)

---

* Equated with the virgin goddess Diana, or Cynthia, with whom the queen was often identified.

FROM AN ENGRAVING BY W. T. FRY
AFTER AN ANONYMOUS PAINTING.
FOLGER LIBRARY.

The so-called Rainbow Portrait of Queen Elizabeth, painted by an unknown artist late in her life. Characteristic of the poetic cult of the ever-beautiful, ageless queen, she is made to appear as a young woman and is surrounded by allegorical symbols of the qualities attributed to her. She was, in fact, vigorous and dynamic to her last illness.

Shakespeare's description of Cleopatra and her barge may have been prompted by the sight of the queen in her royal barge passing up and down the Thames along the Bankside:

> The barge she sat in, like a burnished throne,
> Burned on the water. The poop was beaten gold;
> Purple the sails, and so perfumed that
> The winds were lovesick with them; . . .
> . . . For her own person,
> It beggared all description.

(Antony and Cleopatra II. ii. 237–45)

FROM VISSCHER,
"LONG VIEW OF LONDON."
FOLGER LIBRARY.

The royal barge on its way upriver toward Whitehall, as seen from the Bankside near the Swan playhouse. The sight must have been a familiar one to Shakespeare.

Queen Elizabeth died at Richmond Palace on March
24, 1603. Shortly before her death Shakespeare's company had performed for her at Richmond. "Down is
that Sun which oft did shine so bright," wrote one of
her subjects. Shakespeare, writing later of Cleopatra,
put it this way:

> Finish, good lady. The bright day is done,
> And we are for the dark.

(Antony and Cleopatra V. ii. 235–36)

The Swan

The successor to the throne was a cousin of Queen Elizabeth, King James VI of Scotland, who was crowned James I of England. In effect, James united England and Scotland into Great Britain, though the formal Act of Union did not occur until 1707.

FROM JOHN SPEED, *Theatre of the Empire of*
Great Britain (1614).

FOLGER LIBRARY.

A map showing "the Kingdom of Great Britain and Ire-
land," with insets of London and Edinburgh, King James's
capital as James VI of Scotland.

A royal procession passing through Cheapside, London. Although this picture dates from a later period in the seventeenth century, it illustrates the kind of scene witnessed by the London populace at James's coronation. On that occasion Shakespeare and his company marched in royal livery in the coronation procession.

FROM *Histoire de l'entrée de la reine mère* (1639)
IN ESTIENNE PERLIN, *Description des royaulmes*
d'Angleterre et d'Escosse (1775).

FOLGER LIBRARY.

Ten days after James's arrival in London a warrant was issued to prepare a royal patent, or license, for Shakespeare and his associates "freely to use and exercise the Art and faculty of playing comedies, tragedies, histories, interludes, morals, stage plays, & such other like as they have already studied or hereafter shall use or study . . . within their now usual house called Globe." Each of the players was subsequently issued four yards of red cloth for new liveries to march in the coronation procession.

BEATI PACIFICI

FROM THE FRONTISPIECE PORTRAIT IN HIS
COLLECTED *Works* (1616).
FOLGER LIBRARY.

King James I.

King James realized that if he was to succeed as king he had to have peace in the world, and he set about making a treaty with Spain. England's long hostility with that country was formally concluded with

FROM AN ENGRAVING IN ROBERT WILKINSON, *Londina Illustrata* (1819–25).

FOLGER LIBRARY.

Somerset House, where the Spanish Ambassador and his fellow commissioners were entertained during negotiations for the peace treaty of 1604. Shakespeare's company was paid "for waiting and attending on His Majesty's service by commandment upon the Spanish Ambassador at Somerset House the space of eighteen days, viz. *from the ninth day of August 1604 until the twenty-seventh day of the same."*

a treaty in 1604. Shakespeare and his company were "in attendance" upon the Spanish delegation during the negotiations—an opportunity for as keen an observer as Shakespeare to absorb much about statesmen and statecraft.

FROM AN ENGRAVING IN HENDERSON, *James I and VI.*
FOLGER LIBRARY.

The English and Spanish peace commissioners at the conference table, 1604. The British representatives are on the right, with the lord admiral second from the far end of the table, and Robert Cecil, son and successor of Lord Burghley, with the papers and pen before him.

The execution of the Gunpowder Plot conspirators, showing the prisoners being dragged to the place of execution on hurdles, and being hanged, drawn and quartered.

FROM HENDERSON, *James I and VI*. FOLGER LIBRARY.

All was not easy for King James. One group of malcontents even plotted to blow up Parliament with barrels of gunpowder hidden in the cellars at a time when the king was opening Parliament. The leader of the plot was Guy Fawkes. The date of the planned explosion, November 5, 1605, is still celebrated in England as "Guy Fawkes' Day." The apprehension of the conspirators provided another spectacular execution for the crowds.

The new king frequently had players at court for performances there. In the writing of *Macbeth*, Shakespeare paid an elaborate compliment to James in the show of the eight kings of the royal line of Banquo, ancestor of King James (Act IV, scene i). Shakespeare's company was now supreme as the King's Men.

FROM JOHN LESLIE,
De origine, moribus, et rebus gestis Scotorum (1578).
FOLGER LIBRARY.

King James's family tree, showing descent from Banquo.

CHAPTER FIVE

THE RENAISSANCE

Shakespeare's age saw the flowering of the Renaissance in England, that period of renewed interest in classical learning and literature, of concern for the arts and of belief in the goodness of the world that man had inherited. It was also an era of religious controversy, of speculation and wonder, of scientific progress, of discussion of the relations of men and women, of commercial development and of change in almost every aspect of life. Many of these phases of the Renaissance spirit find reflection in Shakespeare's plays.

Shakespeare made the acquaintance of classical literature in grammar school where he encountered the works of the Roman dramatists, Plautus and Terence, and of the Roman poet, Ovid. Later, when he began to write plays of his own, he utilized this acquaintance with the Latin writers. He also turned to other classical authors for plots. One of the most influential of the Greek writers upon Shakespeare, as upon many other Elizabethans, was Plutarch, whose *Lives of the Noble Grecians and Romans,* first published in English in 1579, served as a source for such plays as *Julius Caesar, Antony and Cleopatra* and *Coriolanus.*

THE LIVES
OF THE NOBLE GRE-
CIANS AND ROMANES, COMPARED

*together by that graue learned Philosopher and Historiogra-
pher, Plutarke of Chæronea:*

Translated out of Greeke into French by IAMES AMYOT, Abbot of Bellozane,
Bishop of Auxerre, one of the Kings priuy counsel, and great Amner
of Fraunce, and out of French into Englishe, by
Thomas North.

Imprinted at London by Thomas Vautroullier
and Iohn VVight.
1579.

*Plutarch's Lives of the Noble Grecians and Romans, trans-
lated by Thomas North in 1579, provided a mine from
which many dramatists, including Shakespeare, quarried
plots.*

Because the Renaissance emphasized learning, some scholars became overly learned and displayed pedantry rather than human culture. Shakespeare satirized the pedantic schoolmaster in *Love's Labor's Lost* in the character of Holofernes:

Nathaniel: *Videsne quis venit?*
Holofernes: *Video, et gaudeo.*
. . . .
Moth [aside to Costard]: They have been at a great
    feast of languages and stol'n the scraps,
Costard: O, they have lived long on the alms basket
    of words. I marvel thy master hath not eaten thee
    for a word, for thou art not so long by the head
    as honorificabilitudinitatibus; thou art easier
    swallowed than a flapdragon.

(V. i. 30–42)

Scientific thinkers in Shakespeare's age had begun probing the mysteries of the natural world and trying to solve some of its puzzles. The old notion that the earth was the center of the created universe was giving way to the new discoveries of Copernicus and Galileo that the planets revolve around the sun. Astronomers continued to theorize about outer space, even as astronomers continue today to speculate about mysteries that still elude them. And men still believed in the influence of the stars on the lives of men, the pseudoscience of astrology, as many people in our own age continue to believe in horoscopes.

FROM AN ANONYMOUS
SATIRE, *Pedantius* (1631).
FOLGER LIBRARY.

Elizabethan schoolmasters emphasized the study of Latin, sometimes to the exclusion of other subjects. The picture here is a caricature of this type of teacher, satirized by Shakespeare in Love's Labor's Lost.

FROM SCHOPPER, "PANOPLIA."
FOLGER LIBRARY.

A geographer measuring distances upon a terrestrial globe. On the table is a celestial globe that was of more interest to astrologers who cast horoscopes.

One of the pseudosciences that attracted interest was alchemy, the study of a system that might turn base metals into gold by some chemical process. Ben Jonson wrote a satirical play on the subject called *The Alchemist.*

FROM KONRAD GESNER, *The New Jewel of Health* (1576).
FOLGER LIBRARY.

An alchemist.

Shakespeare's age had not yet shaken off many other popular superstitions of various sorts. The most prevalent of these was the belief in witchcraft. This was an ancient belief, but it had a virulent outbreak in the sixteenth and seventeenth centuries. King James himself wrote a

FROM MATTHEW HOPKINS, *The Discovery of Witches* (1647).

FOLGER LIBRARY.

Seventeenth-century witches with their familiars.

treatise asserting the prevalence—and the malevolence—of witches, a work entitled *Demonology*. The king liked to cross-examine alleged witches on trial for their lives. Many were executed. Shakespeare made dramatic use of witches in *Macbeth,* finding historical justification for them in Holinshed's *Chronicles of England, Scotland, and Ireland*.

DAEMONOLO-
GIE, IN FORME
of a Dialogue,
Diuided into three Bookes.

IN MY DEFENCE · GOD ME DEFEND ·

EDINBVRGH
Printed by Robert Walde-graue
Printer to the Kings Majeſtie. An. 1597.
Cum Privilegie Regio.

The title page of King James's Demonology
(1597).

Witches, ghosts and demons were very real to the people of Shakespeare's age. They also made good "theatre." It is a measure of Shakespeare's dramatic art that we still accept them in his plays today. A prominent modern psychologist has said that the Elizabethans intuitively knew things about human psychology that we are just rediscovering today by other names.

FROM OLAUS MAGNUS, *Historia de gentibus* (1555).
FOLGER LIBRARY.

A witch raising a wind.

FROM RAPHAEL HOLINSHED'S *Chronicles
of England, Scotland, and Ireland* (1577).
FOLGER LIBRARY.

*The encounter of Macbeth and Banquo, dressed as English
gentlemen, with the Weird Sisters, or Witches.*

Shakespeare's contemporaries were also much concerned with establishing a formal science of psychology. The most systematic effort was refined from theory inherited from the Middle Ages about the influence of the four humors (or liquids) in the body. These humors determined a man's disposition. An abundance of blood, for example, produced a sanguine man who was optimistic. Too much choler (yellow bile) made a man choleric or quick to anger. Too much melancholic humor (black bile) made a man gloomy and introspective. Too much phlegm (whitish mucus) made a man phlegmatic or stolid and dull. Shakespeare utilized some of these beliefs in his characterizations. Jaques in *As You Like It,* for example, is a melancholic type; and Robert Burton, in *The Anatomy of Melancholy,* cited

A
TREATISE OF
MELANCHOLIE.

CONTAINING THE CAVSES
thereof, & reasons of the strange effects it worketh
in our minds and bodies: with the phisicke cure, and
spirituall consolation for such as haue thereto ad-
ioyned an afflicted conscience.

*The difference betwixt it , and melancholie with diuerse
philosophicall discourses touching actions, and af-
fections of soule, spirit, and body: the par-
ticulars whereof are to be seene
before the booke.*

By T. Bright Doctor of Phisicke.

Imprinted at London by Thomas Vautrol-
lier, dwelling in the Black-
Friers. 1586.

*Title page of a learned treatise on abnormal psychology
that had two editions in its first year of publication (1586)
and was reprinted in 1613. This was an important source
for Robert Burton's even more popular* Anatomy of Melancholy *(1621).*

Beatrice and Benedick of *Much Ado About Nothing* as examples of the choleric humor.

Related to the characterization of people by their "humors" was the notion of classifying them by age; certain behavior was to be expected at certain stages of growth and decline. Another popular belief was that people were destined to their stations in life from the moment of their birth. Thomas Heywood expressed this idea in his *Apology for Actors* (1612).

> The world's a theatre, the earth a stage,
> Which God and nature doth with actors fill;
> Kings have their entrance in due equipage,
> And some their parts play well and others ill.
> The best no better are (in this Theatre)
> Where every humor's fitted in his kind:
> This a true subject acts, and that a traitor,
> The first applauded, and the last confin'd;
> This plays an honest man, and that a knave,
> A gentle person this, and he be a clown,
> One man is ragged, and another brave,
> All men have parts, and each man acts his own.
>   Then our play's begun
> When we are born and to the world first enter,
> And all find exits when their parts are done.

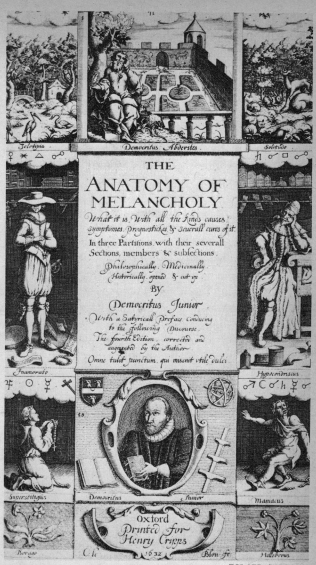

Illustrated title page of the fourth edition of Robert Burton's Anatomy of Melancholy (1632), *showing the various types of melancholia.*

Shakespeare combined the two ideas of the ages of man and the world as a theatre in the famous speech he put in the mouth of melancholy Jaques in *As You Like It*:

> All the world's a stage,
> And all the men and women merely players,
> They have their exits and their entrances,
> And one man in his time plays many parts,
> His acts being seven ages. At first, the infant,
> Mewling and puking in his nurse's arms.
> Then the whining schoolboy, with his satchel
> And shining morning face, creeping like snail
> Unwillingly to school. And then the lover,
> Sighing like furnace, with a woeful ballad
> Made to his mistress' eyebrow. Then a soldier,
> Full of strange oaths and bearded like the pard,
> Jealous in honor, sudden and quick in quarrel,
> Seeking the bubble reputation
> Even in the cannon's mouth. And then the justice,
> In fair round belly with good capon lined,
> With eyes severe and beard of formal cut,
> Full of wise saws and modern instances;
> And so he plays his part. The sixth age shifts
> Into the lean and slippered pantaloon,

FROM A MID-FIFTEENTH-CENTURY WOODCUT IN THE BRITISH
MUSEUM, REPRODUCED IN *Archaeologia*, VOL. 35 (1853).
                                        FOLGER LIBRARY.

*Various "ages of man" found popular reflection in literature
and art. This picture deals with ten ages, each with an
animal symbolic of the particular age.*

With spectacles on nose and pouch on side,
His youthful hose, well saved, a world too wide
For his shrunk shank; and his big manly voice,
Turning again toward childish treble, pipes
And whistles in his sound. Last scene of all,
That ends this strange eventful history,
Is second childishness and mere oblivion,
Sans teeth, sans eyes, sans taste, sans everything.

(II. vii. 149ff.)

The clown, as Heywood observes, was one of the stock roles in the dramas of stage and of life. A favorite device of Renaissance literature was the wise fool—a type of clown who embodied the proverb: "Many a truth is said in jest." The Fool in Shakespeare's *King Lear* is perhaps the most poignant example in dramatic literature.

Shakespeare's age did not believe that all men were born equal or that equality was a good thing for society. Instead, they believed that men and women should be content with the status to which they were born. Exceptional talent and exceptional merit might enable a man to move to a higher status, for English society was not frozen into castes, but men and women were warned not to be discontented with the place in which they found themselves. Instead, they were to labor at their callings for the good of society as a whole. At the very pinnacle of the social order stood the sovereign. Rulers in this day all conceived of themselves as ordained by

FROM MAGNUS, *Historia*.
FOLGER LIBRARY.

A king's fool, or jester.

FROM HOLINSHED'S *Chronicles*.
FOLGER LIBRARY.

The sovereign.

God to rule, and of their subjects as ordained to obey. King James made his views on this subject explicit in the doctrine of divine right. Historians maintain that Shakespeare made Richard III an unmitigated villain in order to justify the usurping of the throne by Henry VII, Queen Elizabeth's grandfather.

Into the mouth of Ulysses in *Troilus and Cressida,* Shakespeare put a great speech on degree which sums up the doctrine of hierarchy:

> Oh, when degree is shaked,
> Which is the ladder to all high designs,
> The enterprise is sick! How could communities,
> Degrees in schools and brotherhoods in cities,
> Peaceful commerce from dividable shores,
> The primogenity and due of birth,
> Prerogative of age, crowns, scepters, laurels,
> But by degree, stand in authentic place?
> Take but degree away, untune that string,
> And hark what discord follows.
>
> (I. iii. 105–14)

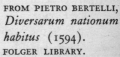

FROM PIETRO BERTELLI,
*Diversarum nationum
habitus* (1594).
FOLGER LIBRARY.

*An English nobleman and
noblewoman as portrayed in a
contemporary costume book.*

The queen was too wise to make an issue of divine right as James did, but she kept her subjects in their places. In a speech at Oxford University in 1592 she had this to say:

I advise you, then, that you go not before the law, but that you follow it. Do not put forth arguments as to whether better laws could be written, but observe what Divine Law commands, and our own law compels. In the second place, remember that each one be obedient to his superior in rank, not by prescribing what ought to be, but by following what has been prescribed. Consider this, that if your superiors begin to do that which is unbecoming, they will have their own superior, by whom they are guided, who ought and will desire to punish them.

FROM SPEED, *Theatrum*.
FOLGER LIBRARY.

An English gentleman and gentlewoman, the place on the social scale to which Shakespeare and his wife were entitled by reason of the coat of arms that Shakespeare procured for his father. It was preferable to be a second-generation gentleman, i.e., "to the manner born."

In Elizabethan England, costumes provided an accurate visual guide to a person's status. Government regulations not only attempted to control extravagance in dress, but set down quite precise limits on fabrics, colors and furs that might be worn by persons of the various social orders. A royal proclamation of 1597, for example, reads as follows:

FROM SPEED, *Theatrum*.
FOLGER LIBRARY.
*A citizen and
a citizen's wife.*

Her Majesty doth straitly charge and command that: None shall wear in her apparel cloth of gold or silver tissued [woven], [or] silk of color purple under the degree of a Countess, except Viscountesses to wear cloth of gold, or silver tissued, in their kirtles [outer petticoats] only.

Sermons were preached "Against Excess of Apparel," and the presumption of dressing beyond one's station was a favorite subject of satire.

FROM SPEED, *Theatrum.*
FOLGER LIBRARY.

A countryman and country-woman, lowest on the hierar-chical scale, but not as lowly as the serfs of some parts of Europe. There were, of course, gradations within each of these major groups.

The progress of business and commerce required the investment of money in large amounts. Some of this capital had to be borrowed. In the Middle Ages, the taking of interest on borrowed money was regarded as a sin, and the debate over the propriety of charging interest continued into Shakespeare's day. Some theologians held that usurers (those who charged excessive interest) were men who had sold their souls to the devil for greed. Gradually, however, businessmen came to accept the charging of moderate interest as the normal way to raise capital. Shakespeare's Shylock, in *The Merchant of Venice,* is an example of a stock character type humanized into a memorable personality.

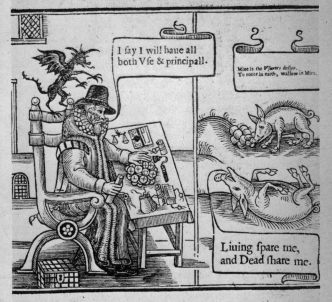

The English Vsurer.

I say I will haue all both Vse & principall.

Mine is the *Vsurers* desire,
To roote in earth, wallow in Mire.

Liuing spare me, and Dead share me.

Caluin Epist. de Vsura.
In repub. benè constitutâ nemo fœnerator tolerabilis est, sed omninò debet è consortio hominum reijci : An Vsurer is not tolerable in a well established Common-weale, but vtterly to be reiected out of the company of men.

FROM JOHN BLAXTON, *The English Usurer* (1634).

A seventeenth-century English moneylender, whom Eliza-bethans were willing to consign to the Devil.

During the Renaissance, women gained freedoms that they had not had in earlier times. In England many women were learned in the classics and other fields of knowledge. Queen Elizabeth could give an extempore speech in Latin. In the business world of London, some women took over the businesses of their deceased husbands and ran them successfully. Foreigners called England "the hell of horses and the paradise of women." Many handbooks of behavior discussed the relations of men and women. But not all authors glorified the "new freedom" of women. Common law still permitted a husband to beat his wife—provided he used a stick no thicker than his thumb. Shakespeare dealt with this theme in *The Taming of the Shrew*, doubtless to the delight of the bachelor apprentices in the audience.

Shakespeare was an author keenly sensitive to the ferment of ideas in his own day. His plays show his utilization of many of these ideas. But he was also aware of universal concepts that are characteristic of all ages, and thus his plays have achieved a permanence not affected by changes in fashions and shifts in ideology.

FROM A POPULAR BROADSIDE (CA. 1620).
COURTESY, THE BRITISH MUSEUM.

Although Shakespeare later portrayed many independent and charming women, his The Taming of the Shrew *illustrates a traditional characterization of women which was often satirical and made to order for a young playwright of limited experience—Kate was one of the earliest of Shakespeare's heroines.*

CHAPTER SIX

THE PUBLICATION OF SHAKESPEARE'S PLAYS

While we know very little about Shakespeare's method of writing, we do know that he wrote rapidly and with great sureness of touch. Ben Jonson commented that he "never blotted a line," meaning that he made few corrections. Some evidence indeed points to hasty writing. But he clearly had a mind that quickly assimilated material that he needed from the best sources that he could find. For example, he got much of his material for the English historical plays from Raphael Holinshed's *Chronicles of England, Scotland, and Ireland*. He sometimes found an old play and reworked it into something new. *The Taming of the Shrew*, in part, at least, was adapted from an older play.

FROM THOMAS HEYWOOD, *Life and Death of Hector* (1614).

FOLGER LIBRARY.

An Elizabethan at his writing table, goose-quill pen in hand.

A playwright in Shakespeare's time simply sold his play to the performing company and thereafter had no copyright or royalty privileges. Sometimes the dramatic companies might sell off copies of used plays to a printer who wanted to publish them. Frequently, however, the dramatic company tried to keep its plays from getting into print. Occasionally a play might be taken down by shorthand, or it might be reconstructed from memory by one or more actors and the resultant copy sold to the printers. Some of Shakespeare's plays, reproduced in this fashion and published in single-play editions, are known as "bad quartos" because of their inaccuracy. The first editions of *Hamlet* and *The Merry Wives of Windsor* are examples of bad quartos.

Plays published singly were in quarto size (that is, a printed sheet folded four times) and are called simply "quartos." The collected editions of plays were brought out in folio size. (A folio sheet is folded twice.)

THE
Tragicall Hiſtorie of
H A M L E T,
Prince of Denmarke.

By William Shakeſpeare.

Newly imprinted and enlarged tó almoſt as much
againe as it was, according to the true and perfeſt
Coppie.

AT LONDON,
Printed by I. R. for N. L. and are to be ſold at his
ſhoppe vnder Saint Dunſtons Church in

Title page of the second quarto edition of Hamlet, *which presented a more accurate version than the "pirated" first quarto.*

Plays at first did not enjoy a reputation as great literature. Ben Jonson was the first English dramatist to have his plays published in a collection called by the

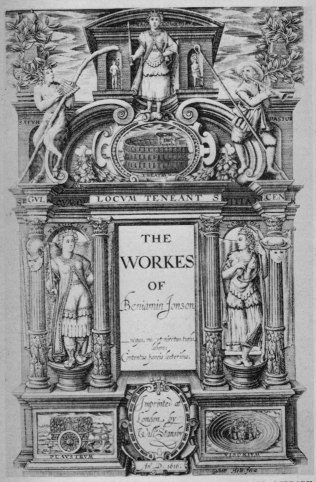

Title page of the first folio edition of Ben Jonson's Works *(1616).*

dignified term of *Works*. Men laughed at Jonson for
having the vanity to call his plays *Works*.

A portrait of Ben Jonson attributed to Isaac Oliver.

The first separate publication from Shakespeare's pen was his narrative poem, *Venus and Adonis* (1593). The first play to be published was *Titus Andronicus* (1594),

VENVS
AND ADONIS

Vilia miretur vulgus: mihi flauus Apollo
Pocula Castalia plena ministret aqua.

LONDON

Imprinted by Richard Field, and are to be sold at
the signe of the white Greyhound in
Paules Church-yard.

1593.

Title page of the first edition of Venus and Adonis
(1593).

which edition has survived in only one copy, now in the Folger Library.

THE
MOST LA-
mentable Romaine
Tragedie of Titus Andronicus:

As it was Plaide by the Right Ho-
nourable the Earle of *Darbie*, Earle of *Pembrooke*,
and Earle of *Suffex* their Seruants.

LONDON,
Printed by Iohn Danter, and are
to be sold by *Edward White* & *Thomas Millington*,
at the little North doore of Paules at the
signe of the Gunne.
1594.

Title page of the only known copy in existence of the first edition of Titus Andronicus *(1594).*

Shakespeare's name first appeared on the title pages of his plays in 1598, when it was carried by the first edition of *Love's Labor's Lost* and the second editions of *Richard II* and *Richard III*.

A
PLEASANT
Conceited Comedie
CALLED,
Loues labors loſt.

As it vvas preſented before her Highnes
this laſt Chriſtmas.

Newly corrected and augmented
By W. Shakeſpere.

Imprinted at London by *W.W.*
for *Cutbert Burby.*
1598.

We know from this title page that Love's Labor's Lost *was presented at court before Queen Elizabeth in the Christmas season of 1597. This was also the first new play to be printed with Shakespeare's name on the title page.*

From that time on, the printing
of Shakespeare's name became more

THE
EXCELLENT
History of the Mer-
chant of Venice.

With the extreme cruelty of *Shylocke*
the Iew towards the saide Merchant, in cut-
ting a iust pound of his flesh. And the obtaining
of *Portia*, by the choyse of
three Caskets.

Written by W. SHAKESPEARE.

Printed by *J. Roberts,* 1600.

Title page of the first quarto edition of The Merchant of
Venice, *emphasizing Shakespeare as author (1600).*

prominent, presumably as his reputation grew.

SHAKE-SPEARES

SONNETS.

Neuer before Imprinted.

AT LONDON
By *G. Eld* for *T. T.* and are
to be solde by *William Aspley.*
1609.

*Title page of the first edition of Shakespeare's Sonnets,
supposed to have been published surreptitiously without
the author's permission. The typographical prominence of
Shakespeare's name probably suggests the growth of his
reputation.*

Not all of Shakespeare's plays were published during his lifetime; the King's Men quite understandably protected their investment. After the playwright's death (1616), two of his former associates in the theatre, John Heminges and Henry Condell, brought together thirty-six of his plays and published them in the first collected edition, known as the First Folio of 1623.

During the seventeenth century three other folio editions of the plays were published. One play, *Pericles,* not included in the Folio of 1623, is now generally attributed to Shakespeare and is included in modern editions of his works.

Mr. WILLIAM
SHAKESPEARES
COMEDIES,
HISTORIES, &
TRAGEDIES.

Published according to the True Originall Copies.

LONDON
Printed by Isaac Iaggard, and Ed. Blount. 1623.

Title page of the first collected edition of Shakespeare's plays, the Folio of 1623.

Editors and authors then were not as careful about reading proof and making corrections as are modern writers. Someone at the press usually looked over the pages as they came from the press and marked such corrections as might be needed. In the meantime the printers were continuing to print off uncorrected pages, which they did not discard. By the time the press was stopped and corrections were made, many pages containing the errors might have been printed. That explains variations in copies of the same edition of an author's works.

The first play in the 1623 edition is *The Tempest,* possibly the last complete play written by Shakespeare. In the scene in which Prospero, exiled Duke of Milan, breaks his magic staff, students of Shakespeare have seen a symbolic act suggesting the dramatist's own retirement and farewell to his art:

> But this rough magic
> I here abjure; and when I have required
> Some heavenly music (which even n~~~ ~ ~
> To work mine ~~ ~   ~~ now I do)
> ~~ ~~ ~~~ cna upon their senses that
> This airy charm is for, I'll break my staff,
> Bury it certain fathoms in the earth,
> And deeper than did ever plummet sound
> I'll drown my book.
>
> (V. i. 57–64)

FROM SCHOPPER, "PANOPLIA."
FOLGER LIBRARY.

Sixteenth-century printers at work. Note the folio pages on the press, with pages already printed stacked for folding.

CHAPTER SEVEN

SHAKESPEARE'S RETURN TO STRATFORD

About 1611, Shakespeare evidently decided that he was wealthy enough to retire from active life in the theatre. He went back to Stratford to lead the life of a retired gentleman, highly respected by his fellow townsmen. But Shakespeare did not completely abandon playwriting. Some of his later plays, including *The Tempest,*

Cymbeline and *The Winter's Tale,* were composed after 1611. They reflect a serenity that suggests Shakespeare's contentment with the quiet life in Stratford.

Trinity Church in autumn.

As early as 1597, Shakespeare had succeeded so well in London that he was able to buy one of the finest houses in Stratford for his family, a house built by Sir Hugh Clopton, a Stratford man who had gone to London and become lord mayor. This house, known as New Place, with a beautiful garden laid out in Sir Hugh's time, was torn down in the eighteenth century, but the garden still exists and is maintained as a showplace. During the summer it blazes with flowers that Shakespeare would have known.

That Shakespeare, like Englishmen ever since, loved his garden, is apparent in the many allusions in his plays to a multitude of flowers and herbs—allusions that reveal the knowledge and sensitivity of a true gardener:

> Here's flow'rs for you;
> Hot lavender, mints, savory, marjoram;
> The marigold, that goes to bed wi' the sun
> And with him rises weeping. These are flow'rs
> Of middle summer, and I think they are given
> To men of middle age.
>
> (*The Winter's Tale* IV. iv. 121–26)

Probably the most famous of Shakespeare's passages on flowers is in Ophelia's mad scene in *Hamlet*:

There's rosemary, that's for remembrance.
Pray you, love, remember. And there is pansies,
that's for thoughts. . . . There's fennel for you,
and columbines. There's rue for you, and here's
some for me. We may call it herb of grace o'
Sundays. O, you must wear your rue with a
difference! There's a daisy. I would give you
some violets, but they withered all when my
father died.

(IV. v. 190–99)

FROM A PHOTOGRAPH.
FOLGER LIBRARY.

The gardens of New Place today.

Early in 1616 Shakespeare's health was failing and on March 25, 1616, he made out his will. To his daughter Susanna, who had married a prosperous physician, Dr. John Hall, he left his land and houses—following the custom of keeping the bulk of an estate intact in the possession of one heir. To his daughter Judith, who had married a vintner, Thomas Quiney, he left the sum of £300, and to other relatives and friends, including several of the King's Men, he left small gifts. To his wife Anne, who already had certain dower rights in his property, he specified a bequest of his "second best bed." A few writers have made much of this and have implied that Shakespeare thus showed a disregard for Anne. The specification more likely was meant to insure that Anne got a bed that she particularly liked.

REPRODUCED IN SIDNEY LEE,
Life of Shakespeare (1899).
FOLGER LIBRARY.

"By me William Shakespeare." Signature on his last will and testament.

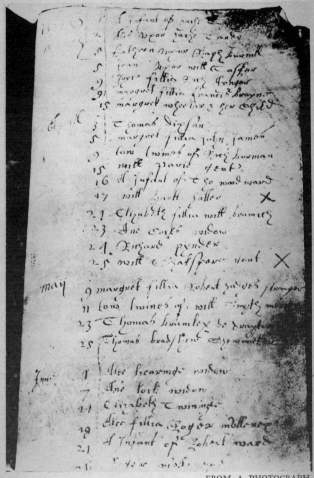

*The entry of Shakespeare's burial, April 25, 1616, in the
Parish Register of Stratford. Note the designation: "Willm
Shakespeare, gent."*

On April 23, 1616, Shakespeare died, and on April
25 he was buried within the chancel of Trinity Church,
a place of honor befitting one of Stratford's most important citizens. On August 6, 1623—the year the First
Folio was published—his wife, Anne, died and was
buried by his side. Sometime in the interim a monument had been erected on the north wall of the chancel
just east of the door to the charnel house. The monument and door may be seen today in Trinity Church;
the charnel house was removed about 1800. The monu-
mental bust, typical of such effigies in the period, is
disappointing as a portrait, yet it is the only likeness in
addition to the engraving in the First Folio that has
any validity.

Shakespeare's death, thirteen years after that of the
great queen, marked the end of an era of magnificent
literature and phenomenal accomplishment for the
English nation. Ever since, men have looked back
upon this period as England's Golden Age.

> Our revels now are ended. These our actors,
> As I foretold you, were all spirits and
> Are melted into air, into thin air;
> And, like the baseless fabric of this vision,
> The cloud-capped towers, the gorgeous palaces,
> The solemn temples, the great globe itself,
> Yea, all which it inherit, shall dissolve,
> And, like this insubstantial pageant faded,
> Leave not a rack behind. We are such stuff
> As dreams are made on, and our little life
> Is rounded with a sleep.
>
> (*The Tempest* IV. i. 167–77)

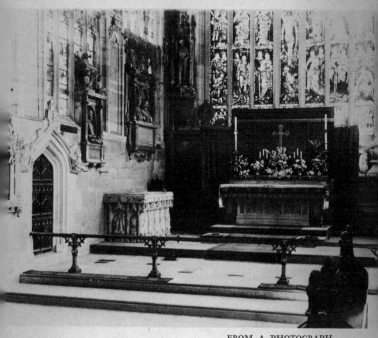

FROM A PHOTOGRAPH.
FOLGER LIBRARY.

*A modern view of Shakespeare's grave and monument in
the chancel of Holy Trinity Church, Stratford.*

EPILOGUE:

SHAKESPEARE'S REPUTATION

Shakespeare's contemporaries paid him great respect, and authors who had known him wrote tributes to him. Some of these tributes appeared in the First Folio of 1623:

> Sweet swan of Avon! what a sight it were
> To see thee in our waters yet appear,
> And make those flights upon the banks of Thames
> That so did take Eliza and our James!
> But stay, I see thee in the Hemisphere
> Advanc'd and made a constellation there!
> Shine forth, thou Star of Poets, and with rage,
> Or influence, chide, or cheer, the drooping Stage;
> Which, since thy flight from hence, hath mourn'd
>   like night,
> And despairs day, but for thy Volume's light.
>
>   (Ben Jonson, "To the Memory of My
>   Beloved, the Author")

Shakespeare's plays, popular in his own time, have never ceased to attract audiences and readers. Thousands of editions have been printed in English, and his plays have been translated into most of the languages of the world. Theatres throughout the world have continued to stage performances of the plays. In the latter part of the seventeenth century, after the Restoration of Charles II and the resumption of play production in London, Shakespeare was one of the most popular of the playwrights from the previous age. Sometimes his plays were rewritten and adapted to suit changed tastes, but they were rarely so changed that Shakespeare's genius was not apparent.

During the eighteenth century, a noted producer and actor, David Garrick, made Drury Lane Theatre famous for the productions of Shakespeare's plays. In Garrick's productions, most of the plays were performed in "modern dress," that is, the dress of Garrick's own time.

FROM AN ENGRAVING AFTER A PAINTING BY JOHN ZOFFANY.
FOLGER LIBRARY.

David Garrick and Hannah Pritchard as Macbeth and Lady Macbeth. Characteristically, they played the roles in costumes of their own day, though Garrick did a later production in Highland dress.

Garrick's worship of Shakespeare
led him to organize and stage a
Shakespeare Jubilee in September of

We ne'er shall look upon his like again.

The Man that
hath no Music
in himself is
fit for Treasons &

SHAKES

the 6.th a

at Strat

This TICKET

The

DEDIC

And to the Great

1769 at Stratford. This was an elaborate celebration with visitors swarming to Stratford from all England.

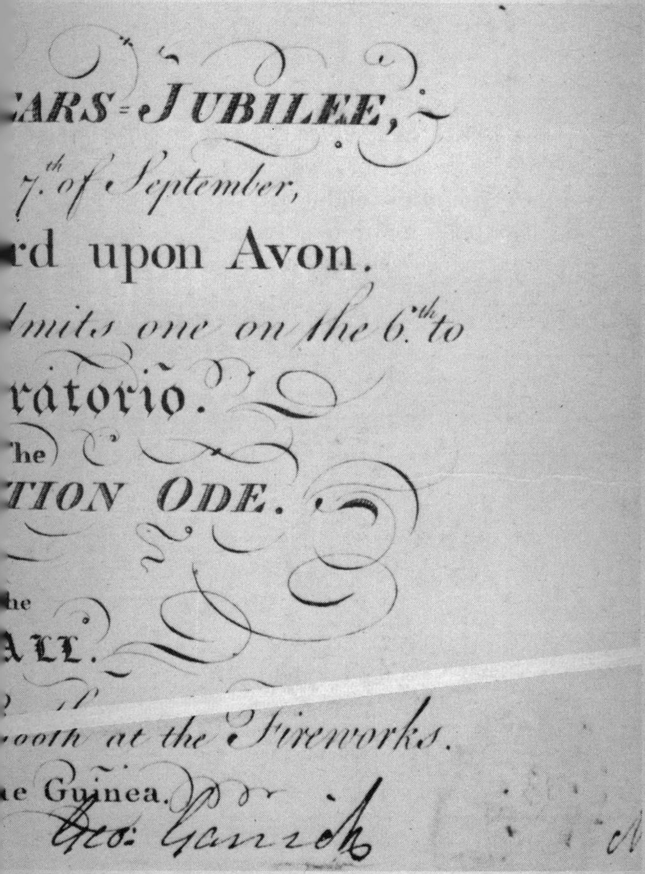

ARS = JUBILEE,
7.th of September,
rd upon Avon.
lmits one on the 6.th to
ratorio.
he
TION ODE.
he
ALL.
ooth at the Fireworks.
e Guinea.
Geo: Garrick

FROM THE HALLIWELL-PHILLIPPS COLLECTIONS.
FOLGER LIBRARY.

A ticket of admission, signed by Garrick himself, to the first day of the Jubilee of 1769.

Actors impersonated the various characters in the plays, and Garrick himself read an ode to Shakespeare. The festivities lasted for two days, but a rainstorm caused the Avon to rise and it very nearly washed away the pavilion built for the occasion. This Jubilee was the first of many elaborate observances held in the years since 1769.

FROM AN ENGRAVING PUBLISHED BY
JOHNSON AND PAYNE (1770).
FOLGER LIBRARY.

At Garrick's Jubilee at Stratford in 1769, one of the attractions was the impersonation of all the characters in Shakespeare's plays by the best actors that Garrick could recruit. This portrayal was later reproduced at Drury Lane Theatre. The principal characters in that procession are shown here.

FROM AN ENGRAVING BY CAROLINE WATERS
AFTER A PAINTING BY ROBERT EDGE PINE (1782).
FOLGER LIBRARY.

David Garrick reciting his Ode to Shakespeare *at the Jubilee of 1769.*

Other eighteenth-century actors besides Garrick found in Shakespeare favorite roles. By modern standards, some of these actors and their costumes were more exotic than convincing.

FROM AN ENGRAVING IN THE
HALLIWELL-PHILLIPPS COLLECTIONS.
FOLGER LIBRARY.

A scene showing James Quin, famous eighteenth-century actor, in the part of Coriolanus. The costume of the hero was probably Quin's own concept of a Roman general's uniform.

In every succeeding age, actors have made their reputations playing parts from Shakespeare. Hamlet has always been a favorite role, and it is every actor's ambition to play that part. In America in the mid-nineteenth century, Edwin Booth, brother of John Wilkes Booth (assassin of Abraham Lincoln), distinguished himself as Hamlet, as did several other American actors.

FROM A LITHOGRAPH.
FOLGER LIBRARY.

Edwin Booth in his celebrated interpretation of Hamlet.

In the nineteenth century, scene painters tried to reproduce realistic settings for the plays and sometimes almost eclipsed the actors in their elaborate pictorial sets. This period also produced a number of talented English actors. Theatregoers could feast their eyes on

The banquet scene of Macbeth *as performed by Sir Henry Irving and Ellen Terry.*

fanciful stage scenery as well as witness skillful inter-
pretations of Shakespeare's characters. Two of the most
noted interpreters of Shakespeare in the last third of
the nineteenth century were Ellen Terry and Sir Henry
Irving.

FROM A PEN AND INK DRAWING BY JOHN JELLICOE.
FOLGER LIBRARY.

Another famous pair, in the early twentieth century, was the husband-and-wife team of E. H. Sothern and Julia Marlowe, shown here in the balcony scene of *Romeo and Juliet.*

FROM A PHOTOGRAPH.
FOLGER LIBRARY.

Julia Marlowe and E. H. Sothern in the balcony scene from Romeo and Juliet.

One of the greatest names in the history of the theatre is that of the French actress Sarah Bernhardt—"the divine Sarah"—who reversed the practice of Shakespeare's time, when men played women's roles, by herself playing the role of Hamlet. She won more renown, however, as Cleopatra.

FROM A PHOTOGRAPH.
FOLGER LIBRARY.

"The divine Sarah" Bernhardt *as Cleopatra in* Antony and Cleopatra.

In our own time, the Old Vic Company of London and the Royal Shakespeare Company of Stratford (England) have been preeminent in Shakespearean production. As in Shakespeare's own company, they have emphasized all-around professional versatility, instead of the cult of one or two great stars.

FROM A PHOTOGRAPH.
FOLGER LIBRARY.

Malvolio's discomfiture in a scene from an Old Vic production of Twelfth Night.

In this century, too, the motion picture screen has given another dimension to Shakespeare. No longer need the Prologue apologize for the limitations of

> . . . this unworthy scaffold to bring forth
> So great an object. Can this cockpit hold
> The vasty fields of France? Or may we cram
> Within this wooden O the very casques
> That did affright the air at Agincourt?
>
> (*Henry V* Prologue. 11–15)

The elaboration of nineteenth-century stage sets has been superseded by realistic as well as impressionistic scenes in movies. The most popular single movie pro-

FROM A PHOTOGRAPH.
FOLGER LIBRARY.

A scene from the Universal Pictures production of Henry
V *under the direction of Sir Laurence Olivier, who also
starred as King Henry.*

duction of Shakespeare in our time has been Sir Laurence Olivier's film of *Henry V* in color. After more than twenty years, it continues to be shown. Sir Lau-

FROM A PHOTOGRAPH.
FOLGER LIBRARY.

Louis Calhern as the mortally wounded Caesar in the Joseph L. Mankiewicz production of Julius Caesar, *which also starred James Mason, Sir John Gielgud and Marlon Brando.*

rence's *Hamlet*, a *Julius Caesar* by Joseph L. Mankie-wicz, and Franco Zeffirelli's *Romeo and Juliet* have also achieved wide critical and popular acclaim.

FROM A PHOTOGRAPH. COURTESY OF
PARAMOUNT PICTURES; COPYRIGHT © 1968 BY
PARAMOUNT PICTURES CORPORATION.

Franco Zeffirelli's production of Romeo and Juliet.

Artists also have found in Shakespeare themes for drawings and painting. Some of their artistic conceptions have influenced stage productions. In the second half of the eighteenth century John Boydell, a London publisher and print-seller, enlisted the best artists of his day to paint scenes from Shakespeare's plays and thus created his remarkable Shakespeare Gallery. Engravings from these pictures were used to illustrate his edition of Shakespeare's dramatic works. Because of near-bankruptcy brought on by the French Revolution, Boydell had to sell his gallery of pictures, which have since been scattered.

FROM AN ENGRAVING BY W. C. WILSON
AFTER THE PAINTING BY R. WESTALL
FOR THE BOYDELL SHAKESPEARE GALLERY (1799).
FOLGER LIBRARY.

Lady Macbeth: Out, damned spot! out, I say!

The great eighteenth-century portrait painter, George Romney, suggests composition and action, and the supernatural quality of Banquo's ghost, in this sketch for Act III, scene iv of *Macbeth*.

Macbeth: Avaunt, and quit my sight!

THE BANQUET SCENE AS SKETCHED BY GEORGE ROMNEY.
FROM A ROMNEY SKETCHBOOK.
FOLGER LIBRARY.

Similarly, a drawing in charcoal by Ary Scheffer evokes the atmosphere of mysterious foreboding in Macbeth's first encounter with the "secret, black, and midnight hags."

All hail, Macbeth, that shalt be King hereafter!

FROM AN ORIGINAL CHARCOAL DRAWING BY
ARY SCHEFFER (N.D.).
FOLGER LIBRARY.

The nineteenth-century caricaturist and illustrator, George Cruikshank, specialized in studies of Shakespeare's great comic character Sir John Falstaff, of the *Henry IV* plays and *The Merry Wives of Windsor*.

Falstaff is dumped into the river "hissing hot."

FROM A WATERCOLOR BY GEORGE CRUIKSHANK.

FOLGER LIBRARY.

In a different vein, the style of another famous illustrator, Arthur Rackham (early twentieth century), captured the ethereal qualities of Ariel and Puck in *The Tempest* and *A Midsummer Night's Dream*.

FROM THE ORIGINAL WATERCOLOR.
FOLGER LIBRARY.

Puck, of A Midsummer Night's Dream, *as conceived by Arthur Rackham.*

In yet another medium, sculptress Brenda Putnam produced a memorable Puck who, facing the United States Capitol, proclaims:

Lord, what fools these mortals be!

(*A Midsummer Night's Dream* III. ii. 116)

FOLGER LIBRARY.

Brenda Putnam's marble statue of Puck, looking toward the Capitol from the west side of the Folger Shakespeare Library, Washington, D. C.

The idea of even-handed justice, seasoned with mercy, is suggested in the balance and symmetry of John Gregory's relief sculpture depicting Act IV, scene i of *The Merchant of Venice:*

> The quality of mercy is not strained,
> It droppeth as the gentle rain from heaven
> Upon the place beneath. It is twice blest—
> It blesseth him that gives, and him that takes.

(IV. i. 189–92)

A sculptured scene from The Merchant of Venice *by John Gregory, on the north façade of the Folger Shakespeare Library, Washington, D. C.*

The greatest tribute to William Shakespeare has come from the millions of readers who have found instruction, solace, entertainment and inspiration in his works. Among these, kings, prime ministers, American presidents and almost every major writer in the Western world have acknowledged their indebtedness to Shakespeare's understanding of human nature and of the writer's art.

THE

DRAMATIC WORKS

OF

William Shakspeare.

FROM THE TEXT OF THE

CORRECTED COPIES OF STEEVENS AND MALONE,

WITH

A LIFE OF THE POET,

BY CHARLES SYMMONS, D. D.

THE SEVEN AGES OF MAN;

EMBELLISHED WITH ELEGANT ENGRAVINGS.

AND A

GLOSSARY.

COMPLETE IN ONE VOLUME.

New-York:

PUBLISHED BY JAMES CONNER.

SOLD BY COLLINS & HANNAY; COLLINS & CO.; C. & G. & H. CARVILL; J. LEAVITT; JOHN DOYLE; JAMES E. BETTS; HENRY C. SLEIGHT, NEW-YORK.—RICHARDSON, LORD, & HOLBROOK; CARTER & HENDEE, BOSTON.—KEY, MIELKE, & BIDDLE, PHILADELPHIA.—FIELDING LUCAS, JR., BALTIMORE.

1835.

FROM LINCOLN'S PERSONAL COPY.
FOLGER LIBRARY.

Abraham Lincoln read Shakespeare and the Bible and was influenced by both. His signature on the title page of Shakespeare's Works *(1835) can be seen faintly at the top of this photograph.*

Ambition.

Brutus in J. Caesar of Shakespeare.

It's a common Proof
that Lowliness is young Ambition's Ladder
Whereto the Climber upwards turns his Face:
But when he once attains the Upmost round,
He then unto the Ladder turns his Back,
Looks in the Clouds, Scorning the base degrees
By which he did ascend. So Caesar may.

I have no Autograph Signature to spare, but the above
is in the handwriting of John Adams.

FROM THE ORIGINAL MANUSCRIPT.
FOLGER LIBRARY.

Brutus's lines on ambition, from Julius Caesar, *copied for his own use by John Adams, second president of the United States.*

Shakespeare.

Others abide our question. Thou art free.
We ask and ask — Thou smilest and art still,
Out-topping knowledge. For the loftiest hill
Who to the stars uncrowns his majesty,
Planting his steadfast footsteps in the sea,
Making the heaven of heavens his dwelling-place,
Spares but the cloudy border of his base
To the foil'd searching of mortality;
And thou, who didst the stars and sunbeams know,
Self-school'd, self-scann'd, self-honour'd, self-secure,
Didst tread on earth unguess'd at. — Better so!
All pains the immortal spirit must endure,
All weakness which impairs, all griefs which bow,
Find their sole speech in that victorious brow.

Matthew Arnold

FOLGER LIBRARY.

A famous sonnet on Shakespeare by the nineteenth-century English writer Matthew Arnold, in the author's handwriting.

Shakespeare, as we have seen, was not without honor in his own country and time. Opposite the engraved title page of the First Folio of 1623, Ben Jonson, a

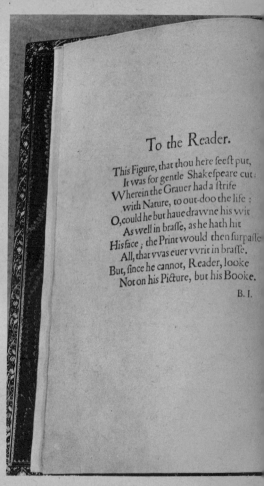

To the Reader.

This Figure, that thou here seest put,
    It was for gentle Shakespeare cut;
Wherein the Grauer had a strife
    with Nature, to out-doo the life :
O, could he but haue drawne his wit
    As well in brasse, as he hath hit
His face ; the Print would then surpasse
    All, that was euer writ in brasse.
But, since he cannot, Reader, looke
    Not on his Picture, but his Booke.

B. I.

Ben Jonson's admonition to the reader of Shakespeare's Works. *Jonson implies that the engraved portrait, the most authentic likeness that we have, is a true one, but that the*

celebrated author in his own right, paid tribute to Shakespeare's wit and enjoined readers to concentrate upon his book. Readers of every time and clime since

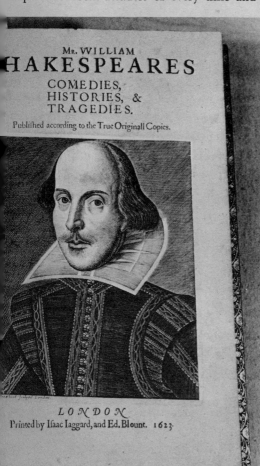

MR. WILLIAM
HAKESPEARES
COMEDIES,
HISTORIES, &
TRAGEDIES.

Published according to the True Originall Copies.

LONDON
Printed by Isaac Iaggard, and Ed. Blount. 1623.

FROM A COPY OF THE FIRST FOLIO OF 1623.
FOLGER LIBRARY.

reader will be much more rewarded by reading the book than by looking for "gentle Shakespeare" in his picture.

have taken that advice, and Shakespeare's plays have followed men even to the battlefield.

Shakespeare would have been pleased could he have known that his plays have been thus applauded by the audiences of the whole globe, season after season. His own hopes, as expressed in his valedictory epilogue to *The Tempest,* were more modest:

> And my ending is despair
> Unless I be relieved by prayer,
> Which pierces so that it assaults
> Mercy itself and frees all faults.
> As you from crimes would pardoned be,
> Let your indulgence set me free.

(Epilogue. 15-20)

Thus simply, from the pen of a gentle man, was the world bequeathed its most prized literary legacy,

By me William Shakespeare.

COURTESY, *Army Times.*

A soldier at the front in Vietnam, 1969, carries into battle a copy of the Folger Library General Reader's Shakespeare edition of The Taming of the Shrew.